# An Educator's Guide to Project-Based Learning

*An Educator's Guide to Project-Based Learning* will inspire practitioners to implement project-based learning effectively and identify the importance of creative and innovative classrooms for highly successful educational outcomes.

Project-based learning is becoming increasingly popular in research and practice. By creating the opportunity to shift from traditional methods of teaching to giving pupils ownership of their learning journey, this highly accessible book takes you through how to implement project-based learning effectively and identifies the importance of creative and innovative classrooms for successful educational outcomes. Dipping into a range of case studies, chapters in this essential resource encourage students to gain confidence when provided with the opportunity to explore their natural curiosity. This book will also highlight how to use project-based learning across different age groups and subject areas, providing readers with insights into new learning environments and the opportunity to learn from others. Each section includes practical examples of how to implement project-based learning and draws on the experiences of educators working in a variety of educational settings.

Covering all the phases, from the early years to Higher Education and Adult Learning, this book will be a key resource for teachers, practitioners, and educational leaders across all the stages of education.

**Fey Cole** is Lecturer in Further and Higher Education, and Teaching and Learning Advisor in the United Kingdom.

# An Educator's Guide to Project-Based Learning
Turning Theory into Practice

Fey Cole

LONDON AND NEW YORK

Designed cover image: © Getty Images

First published 2024
by Routledge
4 Park Square, Milton Park, Abingdon, Oxon OX14 4RN

and by Routledge
605 Third Avenue, New York, NY 10158

*Routledge is an imprint of the Taylor & Francis Group, an informa business*

© 2024 Fey Cole

The right of Fey Cole to be identified as author of this work has been asserted in accordance with sections 77 and 78 of the Copyright, Designs and Patents Act 1988.

All rights reserved. No part of this book may be reprinted or reproduced or utilised in any form or by any electronic, mechanical, or other means, now known or hereafter invented, including photocopying and recording, or in any information storage or retrieval system, without permission in writing from the publishers.

*Trademark notice*: Product or corporate names may be trademarks or registered trademarks, and are used only for identification and explanation without intent to infringe.

*British Library Cataloguing-in-Publication Data*
A catalogue record for this book is available from the British Library

*Library of Congress Cataloging-in-Publication Data*
Names: Cole, Fey, 1984– author.
Title: An educator's guide to project-based learning : turning theory into practice / Fey Cole.
Description: First edition. | New York : Routledge, 2024. | Includes bibliographical references and index.
Identifiers: LCCN 2023041321 (print) | LCCN 2023041322 (ebook) | ISBN 9781032543291 (hbk) | ISBN 9781032543284 (pbk) | ISBN 9781003424345 (ebk)
Subjects: LCSH: Project method in teaching.
Classification: LCC LB1027.43 .C65 2024 (print) | LCC LB1027.43 (ebook) | DDC 371.3/6—dc23/eng/20231023
LC record available at https://lccn.loc.gov/2023041321
LC ebook record available at https://lccn.loc.gov/2023041322

ISBN: 978-1-032-54329-1 (hbk)
ISBN: 978-1-032-54328-4 (pbk)
ISBN: 978-1-003-42434-5 (ebk)

DOI: 10.4324/9781003424345

Typeset in Galliard
by Apex CoVantage, LLC

# Contents

*Acknowledgements* vii

Introduction 1

1 What is project-based learning? 5

2 Developing a project-based learning culture 15

3 Growing as an educator through project-based learning 26

4 Developing spaces that embrace flow and curiosity for learning 33

5 Scaffolding learning through project-based learning 41

6 Overcoming barriers when implementing project-based learning 46

7 Widening students' community and experiences 56

8 Project-based learning in early years 64

9 Project-based learning in primary schools 69

10 Project-based learning in secondary schools 74

11 Project-based learning in further and higher education 80

12 Developing your own sustainable project-based learning
   experiences                                                     87

13 Celebrating the successes and achievements that have
   been made through project-based learning                        100

   Conclusion                                                      109

   *References*                                                    *113*
   *Index*                                                         *118*

# Acknowledgements

I feel very humbled to have been able to get my second academic book to publication and would like to begin my gratitude by thanking my editor, Alison Foyle, for her support throughout the process. This thanks extends to all the Routledge team. To everyone who has taken the time to be interviewed, shared their story, and engaged with my research: Thank you. It is a busy life for educators, and I appreciate your contribution.

When I decided to send off my proposal for this book, I checked in with my mum, Fiona Johnstone-Clark, to ensure she would be agreeable to helping me with proofreading and providing her opinion on my work as I progressed. I thank you, mum, for agreeing without hesitation and for being my advocate in everything I do. She has been a role model throughout my life and has always had my back. In my conclusion to this book, I write about a very special place, and I am grateful for the many times we have been able to go there together and find peace, happiness, and solace. Home is where we are.

This book is built on many years of experience, and I am thankful for the friends and connections that have been made throughout that journey. Most importantly, I would like to dedicate this book to all the students that I have worked with and who I will get to work with in the future. They are a continual inspiration and show me the good in the world. Their experiences are what this book is built on, and I would like to thank each and every one of them for what they have taught me. When my first book was published, I was blown away by the kindness of student groups and realised how important it is for us to put ourselves forward to try new things. I hope that I can role model to students that all of us can change our direction, embrace new aspirations, and strive for positive change whilst knowing who we are and what values shape us.

For many years now, I have worked at the same further and higher education college, and I would like to thank all of the team there for their trust, commitment, and values. I have been trusted and encouraged over the years to become involved in new opportunities, and this freshness and innovation have led to much growth, along with friendships that mean a great deal to me.

In this book, I talk a lot about connections with nature and the importance of how we create physical environments. In the times where I have been incredibly busy, transitioning between my employment and writing, I want to thank my buddy Scruffy, a loyal and energetic Cairn Terrier, for his companionship. He has sat on my lap as I make notes, perched on a chair next to me as I meet with people online, and reminded me to take a break and get outside as required. There is something rather lovely about the excitement that comes every morning to mark a new day starting, and this excitement is maintained whenever a new chapter of the day begins.

I am grateful to the community of Dungannon for making us feel at home many years ago and continuing to do so since. I may still have my London accent, but I am most certainly a proud Dungannon woman, and I am thankful for the many friends that have since become family. I hope to showcase some of the exceptional work that takes place in Northern Ireland through the platforms I use, and it is wonderful to be able to work and share time with so many amazing individuals. I would like to thank my mother-in-law, Elizabeth Cotterell, for all her support and love. We are glad that the children have Granny on their doorstep.

As in everything I do, I could not do it without the love and understanding of the rest of the Coles. Richard, thank you for being a true partner and for making me happy. You always remind me of the importance of balance, and I am glad that our family is always what comes first for both of us. To my darling children, Ruby, Matilda, and Henry: You are my world. Dream big, take breaks, and be proud. Keep asking questions that make you curious, especially when there's an awkward silence. Everyone needs a bit of craic each day.

To you, the reader, I am so appreciative of you, and I hope that the book helps you on your own journey. This book is for everyone who strives to bring education to life and who wants students to fall in love with learning. Please do get in touch through social media; I would love to hear what the next chapter brings for you!

# Introduction

I have worked in education for many years now. My expectations are that I will work in education for many more years to come. Teaching brings me much happiness each day, and the students I work with remind me daily of the importance of challenging oneself and striving to be a continual learner. I wrote this book as an educator, someone who is within the classroom each working day and can appreciate the challenges and restrictions that our profession can face. For you, dear reader, my intentions are to provide a guide to project-based learning (PBL) that will consider the day-to-day pressures and requirements that are expected from us whilst also focusing on the innovation and creativity that bring fulfilment to our practice. I would like to start this book by sharing a story that changed my practice and led to me embedding PBL opportunities into more areas of the curriculum I cover.

A student group I was working with was involved in a PBL activity that required them to bring together community groups to support intergenerational practice and explore how we develop learning spaces that not only bring learning opportunities for primary-aged children but also seek to tackle how we minimise feelings of isolation for senior adults in our society. It was early on in our journey with this project, but it had already proven highly engaging for students and an exciting way to open up our college doors to the wider community. I felt as though I had already handed the reins over to students and was purely facilitating rather than leading them into their choices and decisions. I think I was nearly there, but then something happened that changed me as a lecturer and made me realise I still had some way to go before I was completely student-focused in my pedagogical approach.

I had just had my first opportunity to move into a management role. I was really enjoying it, but it required me to move across locations, and on the day in question, where I had expected a full day of planning our sessions with the student group, I was called to another campus. I felt completely torn. If I was not with the group that day, then the next practical day, where students would implement their plans, would need to be cancelled. The problem was that I had no choice but to leave class. I had 45 minutes free and made the decision that honesty was the best way forward (it always is!) and took my sticky

DOI: 10.4324/9781003424345-1

situation to the student group. There were options. I needed to tell them what they were.

Of course, as soon as I walked in, there was much excitement about the plans that they had come up with. My heart dropped; I did not want to dampen this energy and creativity. I called a round-table discussion and laid my cards on the table. We had the teacher's cover sorted for their day of lessons. We explored the options together. They could cancel the next session, and we could leave it until next month. They could get other coursework completed with support from the cover teacher. I also had one last option. They could get it planned independently, check in with me on emails, and it could still go ahead. It would mean taking on my responsibilities, like contacting other departments to sort out hospitality arrangements, talking to the caretakers about what layout we needed for the space, and making sure the room was booked accordingly. Of course, they went with the final option. They suggested it before I did. They had it covered. They promised they would be professional and keep me updated, gaining advice if needed. I had to trust in them completely. I felt quite nervous, but I also knew I had full confidence in their knowledge and ability.

By the time I had got myself down to my next spot and sorted, I checked my emails. I could feel the excitement in the messages. They had spoken with colleagues of mine, got things booked, come up with new ideas they wanted to run past me, and managed much more than I would have done if I had been facilitating the session. Without me there, they had taken full ownership of the project and worked cohesively together as a team. The dynamic of the classroom environment changed that day; there had been no hierarchy, and I had been a very basic project manager on a working team's project. They were fully submerged into a work-style activity, and the natural and subconscious leadership role that I had held control over as the teacher had been removed. Chance had brought us a magical moment, and in my next session with them, the project that they had planned went perfectly. I was so impressed and proud to know each and every one of them.

What I learned that week was the importance of trust and the need for equal balance between students and educators. There is no denying that I squirmed when they told me they had asked a member of staff to undertake a task for them. The hierarchy can be ingrained in us all without us realising how powerful this chain of command can be. Their requests and instructions had not been out of turn, but they did not meet the usual procedure. It had, however, been asked for professionally and politely and had been met with a very positive response from a colleague. I had not enjoyed walking away from their class and not being able to talk through their ideas with them, but actually, it was a superb lesson. I sound as though I am trying to do myself out of a job here. I am not discrediting the need for educators, but there are times when you have created a learning environment and then have to take a step back for the learning to take place. The students I was working with would soon be moving onto employment; if we cannot trust them to make decisions independently at this stage, then we have not prepared them properly for their next transition. That day changed me as an educator. Prior to that day, I thought I had handed over the reins and that students had full autonomy over their learning experience, but I had not been quite there yet. It took a problem for me to recognise the help I needed and the importance of valuing each of the students' voices.

Since this time, I have continued to develop alongside students and appreciate the opportunity to learn from them. Presenting complicated problems or topics that provoke curiosity has led to a different approach to delivering the curriculum and has brought new ways of thinking that draw on students' experiences and creativity. The more time that I have invested in delivering programmes that embrace PBL, the more I have seen its benefits for students' progression and their recognition as to why it is so valuable, and they embrace developing the skills to be a life-long learner. At the time of writing this book, apprenticeships are taking a shift in Northern Ireland, where I live and work, to further embed PBL into curriculum content due to the way in which PBL prepares students for the workplace, and it is an exciting time to strengthen our approach to ensure that each learner can gain confidence and skills to carry forward.

This book will provide you with the basis for implementing PBL within your provision. Drawing on a range of educators' experiences, you will be able to understand how we embed this approach into our lesson and curriculum plans and widen the opportunities for students to feel autonomy and freedom in their learning. Case studies review different classrooms and age groups, and I would encourage you to read all of the chapters, even if you do not work with the age group discussed, as you will gain insights into other people's practices that can stimulate new thinking as to how you approach your own practice.

Throughout this book, I refer to different types of learners and move between pupils, students, children, and adults. I try to relate the term in relation to the experience upon which I reflect, but this book requires us to think creatively, so no page is shared with the intention of benefitting only one particular category. I also move between the terms 'project-based learning', 'PBL', and 'project-based activities'. All of these are the same approach; they are just referenced differently to suit the paragraph in which I have written. I refrain from talking about *my* students, and you may notice I instead discuss the students I work with. This is important as it is part of removing the power imbalance between educator and student. Students do not belong to me; their own individualism is important to recognise, and I do not want to create an environment where my control is the focus. How we use language is important and can mean the difference between positive space and negative space. I will not pretend there is not the odd slip-up and that my words do not feed into an imbalance at times, but with reflection on how we use our language, we can evaluate this as we progress and be better for the next time. We are all humans, and that makes us lifelong learners. What is important is to be committed to positive change, and I hope that within this book I have used terms that refer to individuals and groups appropriately.

Whether you are an experienced PBL educator or this is new to you, the book will act as a catalyst for fresh thinking and reflecting further on how students can connect with their community and gain a deeper appreciation for what education can bring them. PBL is not about throwing in a project as part of the term but critically reflecting on how it can enhance the learning experience. I take a slow and steady approach to all that I do to ensure that the skills required for the task in hand are developed and that I do not exceed my commitments. PBL is not something to be rushed and slotted in as an unnecessary addition, but instead something where we can enjoy the moment and celebrate creative thinking. Whilst not only preparing students for the path ahead, quality PBL will also encourage individuals to be present in the moment and feel at ease trying something new. As you progress through the book, the expectation is that you will be able to draw on the guidance and experiences of others to evaluate how PBL will work in your own organisations and how it fits within your own approach as an educator.

# 1 What is project-based learning?

It may not be overly surprising that, as an early years educator by vocation, my pedagogy is largely rooted in constructivist theory. As soon as you embark on a journey in the early years sector, the names Montessori, Piaget, and Vygotsky are woven through your child development modules. I am a strong advocate for childhood development to be taught at all levels of teacher training, as there is a lot to gain from understanding how children move through the stages and the complex interactions between different developmental areas. What many of my learning experiences on child development have taught me is that my role as an educator is as a facilitator, observing interactions, reflecting, and providing opportunities to scaffold learning further, something we will review in more detail as we move through this chapter. Although this book is not primarily aimed at early years education, the constructivism theory that early years theorists have been developing for many years is important for all stages of learners, and its influence can be seen throughout the project-based learning approach. In this chapter, we will explore the influence of constructivist theorists and how this correlates to the project-based learning approach.

## What is project-based learning?

Project-based learning brings us closer to the real world. Instead of teachers presenting knowledge and an end result, students are posed with the task of finding solutions to problems alongside their peers, making sense of knowledge as they move through the process of developing projects. By focusing on real-life problems and challenges, students' investigative skills are encouraged, and they are able to develop these and other skills through sustained thinking as they move through the experience. Adopting a student-led approach to learning, each individual will understand their role within the team and will make their own decisions about how they transition through to their end goal, something we will explore further in Chapter 2. As students develop their self-directed learning capabilities, they connect with the wider community to source information in regards to the problem posed. As educators, our role is to introduce the problems we want the students to explore and mentor them through their journey, evaluating what resources and input they require to get

DOI: 10.4324/9781003424345-2

to their final showcase. Project-based learning (PBL) requires teacher input, but it is required in a facilitator and mentor capacity, where we observe and respond to the lead of the students. As we move through this book, we will consider how this looks for different age groups and review how we prepare projects that are beneficial for students' progress. This chapter explores the theory behind the planning and provides us with an understanding of why the project-based approach benefits students and engages them in valuing the purpose of the learning experience. Projects can be small-scale or take place over a long period of time, but what is most important is that the students have ownership of their journey and that the process is authentic. As an educator who uses project-based learning daily and has researched the benefits for other teachers who adopt it within their lessons, I have been able to see the positive outcomes it brings to students as they progress and how it has supported them as they move into adulthood. The theories discussed within this chapter have been instrumental in informing my approach and evaluating the learning that has come from PBL activities.

## The influence of constructivist theory on project-based learning

The constructivist approach is a two-way process. The learner acts upon interests, seeking knowledge to construct their ideas through investigation and discovery, and the educator uses reflection and observation to inform their practice, focusing their planning around the individual rather than curriculum content. This can prove problematic when trying to balance both being student- or child-led and meeting the educational requirements we are governed by within the classroom. Taking time to reflect on the links between curriculum and pupil interest is important for us to develop projects that fit into the frameworks we follow and can support us in developing strong project-based activities that balance this accordingly and keep individuals engaged in their learning experience. When adopting a constructivist approach, we need to let go of the hierarchy dynamic that can come within the classroom, where the adult is perceived as having all of the information. We should instead see ourselves as educators who can guide and facilitate spaces where students can co-construct knowledge alongside the educator and their peers. Freire (2017) believed that culture and knowledge are continually changing, and this acts as a reminder that none of us can hold all the answers. Answers change over time and space. Our role as educators is to support students in making sense of their experiences and to provide them with the skills to become critical thinkers.

The constructivist theory has developed over time and is not a new approach to educational practice. John-Jacques Rousseau, a philosopher during the European Enlightenment period, was a major contributor to how constructivism has evolved and how we see our approach to teaching in the West today. Born in 1712, Rousseau was one of the first modern thinkers to discuss that, within education, children needed authentic experiences rather than being told what to think. Seeing nature as our greatest teacher, Rousseau

(2004) believed that if students were surrounded by nature, this would stimulate their natural curiosity. He also placed value on the learner being placed in situations where they had to solve their own problems, as he believed this was how learning takes place. Rousseau stressed that if a child only learned things by being obedient to the teacher, then they would never do anything for pure enjoyment or look past something that did not provide satisfaction in the present moment they were in. It can be somewhat dissatisfying to read his vision and see that we still have to push back from teaching practice where knowledge is imparted to students and rote learning methods are still commonplace in the classroom.

## Confucius: a moral and ethical teacher

Considered the first teacher of China, Confucius still holds great influence on Eastern teaching practice. Born in (approximately) 551 BCE, his philosophy did not promote literal thinking but instead encouraged deep thought, where a scholar would spend time studying from a variety of resources and using debate amongst their peers to think critically and creatively, seeing this as an essential process for growth. The Confucian philosophy is still highly influential today in China and East Asia, promoting life-long learning as a journey to evolve through time and place, understanding our own character, and feeling confident in our true nature. Confucius did not provide lectures for his students, instead posing questions, and it is said that when he was asked by a student, 'Do you think that my way of acquiring knowledge is simply to study many things and remember them?' The student said, 'Yes, isn't that the case?' Confucius replied, 'No, I have one principle which I use like a thread, upon which to string them all'. Recognising when he made a mistake, Confucius saw this as part of the learning process. Seeing himself as both authentic and creative and placing emphasis on peer learning, Confucius can be seen as the starting point for constructivist theory, and this approach is influential in how we approach projects in the classroom today.

## Jean Piaget and Lev Vygotsky

When understanding and interpreting constructivist theory, Jean Piaget and Lev Vygotsky's theories are central. Both spent time researching how children make sense of the world around them by constructing knowledge and interacting with experiences. Piaget believed that children are at the centre of knowledge creation, and it is from this that the learning process takes place, moving through cognitive stages. Vygotsky's theory built on this and put great emphasis on the need for social interactions to create shared meanings and develop cognitive processes through these interactions. Although there are similarities between both theories, for example, both put great emphasis on how learning takes place through the acquisition of language, they viewed the process of learning differently. Piaget (Huang, 2021) believed that learning took place through children's interactions with the environment and that they would only learn if they accomplished the processes of assimilation, accommodation, and equilibrium (something we will explore a little later in this chapter). Vygotsky viewed social and cultural interactions as the basis of how learning takes place and believed that learning could not be separated from its social context. Developing the theory of the zone of proximal development (ZPD) (again, something we will review later) helps us understand how we can scaffold learners' understanding further to support their development and learning. Both theorists have been widely credited in the field for their work, but it is also important to review how their work has since been built on and where elements of their research have since been discredited. However, returning to their studies provides us with an understanding of how the concept of constructivism has evolved over time.

**Piaget: schemas, assimilation, accommodation, and equilibrium**

Piaget used the term *schemas* to refer to our brains' starting knowledge and cognitive basis. This function can both hinder us and support us in prospering depending on how our brain processes the information and helps us make sense of what we see as important when presented with many different pieces of information. Piaget's cognitive development theory suggests that we build from these schemas to expand children's knowledge and understanding, correcting mistruths that they have developed whilst making sense of the world. An example of a schema could be a young child brought up with a pet rabbit. The rabbit has brown fur, one floppy ear, and a white patch on his back leg. The child has not met any other rabbits and holds the belief that all rabbits are boys, brown with a white patch on their back leg, and have one ear that flops. The child's experiences have led to this schema, and then one day the child's father settles down at bedtime to read the child a story, and the main character in the book is a little black rabbit with two pointy ears. The child's thinking is modified, and there is a shift in their pre-existing schema. Piaget (1964) describes this stage as *assimilation,* when there is an *adaptation* to pre-existing knowledge and the child has to change their thinking in a process of *accommodation*. This process of *accommodation* is where new schemas can develop further and previous ideas can be altered, following new information. *Equilibrium* is the balance between previous and new schemas. In the example of the child and their pet rabbit, they learn that there are variations in the animal; it is not that the little brown rabbit with the patch on his back leg does not exist, but instead there can be differences. As educators, or as the child's father in this example, we can introduce new seeds of thought: Are all rabbits pets? Do they all eat the same food? Are there assumptions the child has about the rabbit that are not actually correct? Piaget (1964) saw the role of the educator as one where we implemented experiences and different materials that would stimulate thinking further and were based around the individual learner. This lends itself well to how project-based learning can be approached through challenging current mindsets and investigating new subjects together as a group.

## Vygotsky's zone of proximal development and collaborative learning

Vygotsky's theory (1978) suggests that children need provision that supports them just above their level in their ZPD, a stage where the child has not yet mastered something but is not out of reach of doing so. Introducing activities just beyond their level of knowledge and understanding is optimal for learning, and Vygotsky (1978) suggests that through educator guidance, learning and progression can take place. Vygotsky's (1978) theory on the ZPD sees children learning from the cultural world around them and recognises that learning is not an individual's isolated effort but instead views that children will learn through collaborative effort. Theorists such as Vygotsky (1978) identified the importance of objects being culturally relevant within activities; examples of cultural tools can include language, symbols, maps, books, and media. Considering the cultural tools we use within projects is an important aspect of our planning, ensuring that individuals can relate to the tools and connect with them. As children learn, their thinking is shaped by the cultural tools around them and the guidance of others. This theory that cognition is not an individual construction is widely recognised by sociocultural theorists, and Vygotsky put great emphasis on the role of social interaction in learning. The use of collaborative learning and the context of the resources are viewed as highly important for developing children's cognitive skills.

Just as we see scaffolding surrounding a building, Vygotsky (1978) put great emphasis on the role of the educator in raising children's experiences so that they could reach optimum levels of learning. Although Vygotsky never used the term *scaffolding*, which was later introduced by Jerome Bruner (1986) when Bruner evaluated the role of teaching in relation to the ZPD, the principles remain similar between the theorists. Like the example used with the rabbit when talking about schemas, where the adult uses open-ended questions and introduces new schemas, Vygotsky and Bruner's work on scaffolding encourages us to evaluate how we can surround the child with opportunities to progress their thinking further. It is not just the educator who can scaffold learning; it is something that takes place when learning collaboratively. As pupils advance their skills, they can actively support one another in learning by talking through their thinking and gaining new knowledge from alternative perspectives. It is important that we consider, as educators, how we can support scaffolding effectively. When we consider the physical scaffolding that leads up to the roof, if a segment is missing from one level, we have the inability to reach the top. Also, if there is not some stretch between each level, it will take us a longer period of time to reach the higher level. There are risks involved, and communication with peers is necessary to ensure our safety, but the risks are worthwhile if we have the required tools to support us.

Supporting learners in sharing their learning experiences as they progress through tasks so that they can scaffold learning through the activities with one another still requires you, as the educator, to facilitate and support the development of these skills. Prompts left on the table that include reflective questions can be useful as a tool to stimulate discussion. Reflecting on how you create a culture where everyone's voice is heard and people feel safe to speak up and share mistakes will also support this. Consider your role in scaffolding learning. How can you shift from instructional teaching to facilitation? Bruner's (1986) research in scaffolding learning and the role adults played in helping the children learn suggested that children co-create knowledge when working in collaborative activities in joint participation with others. When we consider the tools we use to facilitate learning, we would benefit from considering that 'the preoccupation is not the teacher's "instruction", but the child's "*construction*"' (DeVries and Kohlberg, 1990); how the learner processes the knowledge and material that they are presented with supports their development and provides them with the opportunity to explore independent thinking.

Collaborative learning is when two or more people work together to learn new concepts and solve problems together. The collaboration of the group is essential and requires the individuals to listen to one another, and it is through this process that different viewpoints will be heard and those sharing will develop skills to articulate themselves clearly. In a collaborative learning approach, it is noted that knowledge is a social construct, and from this viewpoint, it is suggested that students can collaborate in small groups to exchange knowledge and create meaning from experiences (Oxford, 1997). In project-based learning, collaboration is key for progression, and it is important for students to fully understand the problem that they are being presented with so that they can work together to develop and present a solution. Collaboration can take place in a number of ways and does not need to happen within the classroom. Technology provides us with a variety of avenues for sharing ideas and perspectives, from an online shared whiteboard to messaging and discussion spaces.

## Jerome Bruner: active learning

Jerome Bruner (1986) is often credited with being the theorist behind *discovery learning* pedagogy, a pedagogical approach aligned with constructivism. This approach to learning is based on the principles that students need to discover things for themselves and that the educator needs to provide problem-solving opportunities to build on their past knowledge to make sense of something new. Through students' active engagement, they feel more autonomy over their learning, and the experiences can be tailored to suit the individual. Within this model, the teacher must consider how they present a problem for students to investigate and the resources that will be provided. As the students progress, observation and reflection are required from the educator to follow the students' thinking and evaluate how further scaffolding of their knowledge can be implemented. A flexible approach is required for this, as students may come to the end goal through different mechanisms, so it is important to review progress throughout rather than waiting for an end product to be handed in.

An example of how this may look in the classroom could be if we were delivering a lesson on sustainability. Our learning outcome is to learn more about the impact plastic pollution has on the environment. In a more traditional style of teaching, we may present facts and statistics to students through presentation, video, or oral material and complete some worksheets on different types of material and how long each may take for decomposition to take place. One of the outcomes of this learning will be that plastic does not decompose, instead breaking into smaller pieces, which substantially impacts the environment. If adopting the discovery learning approach, we could begin this lesson with a data collection activity of the waste that is generated over a day in the classroom, with the problem presented of what to do with it to have the least impact on the environment. It could be useful for you to spend ten minutes now jotting down a brainstorm of what resources you may need for this lesson and the thinking this problem may generate. You may wish for students to record their thinking in a variety of ways to show their understanding of the learning outcomes that you hope for them to achieve by the end of the lesson. There are many creative ways to explore this topic, and this could even lead to the implementation of a new recycling system designed by the students for your school, bringing not just learning but also a positive impact on the environment. This also creates a meaningful purpose for students to engage in the topic.

**Education and well-being**

Many of us in education will have explored Maslow's theory (1954) and the need for our basic survival and physiological needs to be met before we can progress onto growth needs. This view means that consideration must be given to areas such as nutrition, sleep, and a sense of security, as these provide individuals with the building blocks to build on their confidence and see their potential. However, it has since been recognised that Maslow's theory was founded on the research he had undertaken when visiting the Blackfoot community (a community located in the River Valley of Saskatchewan, Canada), where he was undertaking his anthropological research. The Blackfoot Framework differs from Maslow's Hierarchy of Needs as it does not view self-actualisation as an individual responsibility but instead as the responsibility of the community. Children are brought up as valued members of society, with their views and contributions appreciated in the same way as those of adults. Emphasis is put on community cooperation within this First Nation framework (Blackstock, 2011), and it is important for resources, wisdom, and trust to be shared amongst all members of society. In Western culture, we often move through life with an individualistic approach; this is why it can prove challenging when we ask students to move from independent work to sharing the load with a team through project-based learning (something we will explore further in Chapter 6 when reviewing barriers to PBL). Our education systems in Western society do not lend themselves to being led by our curiosity and utilising skills that can be used to support a team activity. Instead, we still frequently work to memorise information to prepare ourselves for exams, with one final grade applied for years of contribution. This approach not only loses the advantages of community work, but can also prove exhausting, impacting our emotional health in the process. If we draw from the Blackfoot Framework, we move away from a model where those who fall back are left behind and instead adopt a goose formation, where we drop back and move forward as we work towards our common goal. It prevents one person from having to carry the full load and reminds us to speak up when we are feeling confused or overwhelmed.

## Dewey: leading the way to project-based learning

Project-based learning is a great way for pupils to follow their own interests through intrinsic motivation. Differentiation within the lesson supports deeper investigation, and students are able to see their individual progression. When we are interested in something, the likelihood is that we will challenge ourselves further, and this can be seen as students become more confident in following their interests and feel autonomy over the situation. Project-based learning requires students to find information from a variety of resources and moves away from being directed by the teacher. As students develop their research skills, the accessibility of information is much broader through PBL, and they can find the tools that work most effectively for them. Enriching the resources and exploring new ways to gather information is a positive way to learn together and encourage choice in the approach students will take to their projects. Whether students use books or weblinks or get out into the community to talk to others, there are a range of possibilities that can deepen students' understanding of a topic, providing them with mechanisms for making sense of the information that they find.

Many would consider John Dewey as the creator of project-based learning. Dewey (2011) believed that we learn through 'doing', through experiential and student-directed learning. A strong advocate for lifelong learning, Dewey founded a school in Chicago in 1896, where lessons promoted a collaborative approach amongst pupils. Dewey wanted to find a way where the individual could flourish, developing their own capacities within a group environment. Dewey's University of Chicago Laboratory School was pivotal for the progressive education movement and was not seen as a place where educators would teach through dictation but instead stimulate students' direction through curiosity. Lessons would not teach specific skills at set times, but instead, the classroom was seen as a scientific laboratory, which was underpinned by Dewey's scheme that focused on three components that the educator should be striving towards in unison:

**The psychological:** This component is based on the pupil's interests and their intrinsic motivations. Educators are encouraged to use these natural impulses to develop a child-centred pedagogy where projects are introduced by the teacher and shaped around the pupils' curiosities.
**The sociological:** The environment needs to be a collaborative space where democracy is promoted. Each individual should know their role within the group, and consideration should be given to societal practices and attitudes and how we can be respectful of the collective.
**The logical:** The content and method used within the lessons need to be presented in a logical order to consider how ideas can be strengthened and advance thinking further. Dewey viewed this as instrumental to developing a progressive society.

Dewey viewed democracy as a form of social intelligence, believing that through respecting one another and approaching problems collaboratively, we are able to find common goals and develop ways to work together to build stronger communities and enable individuals to thrive. Whilst the Laboratory school was designed to test Dewey's theories, it was also there to evaluate how active learning could replace the more traditional *chalk and talk* classrooms that were common in Western school systems. Some may view learner-focused practice as one that makes the teacher redundant, but Dewey's view of how educators brought the three principles of his didactic scheme together was an approach where educators worked closely throughout the learning process to bring curiosities into focus and provide direction. Active learning went hand-in-hand with reflection, and Dewey promoted the importance of both students and educators using reflection to give meaning to experiences. By reflecting on the 'doing', individuals are able to evaluate how to overcome problems, a skill required when moving out of education and into vocational roles.

### The influence of education on emotional health

Learning and mental health are interconnected, and we cannot consider one without planning for how we will support the other. Miraei (2005) suggests that learners with low self-esteem may not participate in learning activities as actively as those with higher levels of self-esteem. This could be due to the individuals not believing that they are capable of undertaking the problems they encounter or that they are able to complete the activities set before them. When we design and facilitate a learning experience, it is of the utmost importance that we recognise the emotions that will come along with it and build trusting environments where teams can speak up about the challenges they encounter. When we struggle with our mental health, research suggests that our grades often drop, our anxiety increases, and it can lead to dropping out of school (Eisenberg, Downs and Golberstein, 2009). We need to adopt a fresh approach to education that focuses on self-esteem and provides students with a community where they feel safe to be themselves. There is much more work that needs to go into this area, and our mental health support services require desperate funding measures, but project-based learning does develop a sense of confidence and pride in the process of learning that is not as evident in traditional approaches to teaching. This is my second book on teaching practice, and my first explored the advantages of incorporating intergenerational learning experiences into the classroom environment. Throughout my research into intergenerational learning and project-based learning, the key has been the importance of community and feeling part of it. Students understanding of their environment and feeling that their contributions are recognised can be an incredible tool for supporting their educational journey. This book evaluates the PBL process and the importance of developing stronger connections so that we can develop our knowledge and learning further. The underpinning theories discussed in this chapter are not exclusive to project-based learning, and there are also other theories that will influence educators as to how they incorporate projects into their lessons, but this chapter provides us with a starting point to delve deeper into why project-based learning can be an effective mechanism for engaging students and creating authentic learning experiences. As you continue through the book, you will find further research and theoretical perspectives introduced, and I would encourage you to evaluate how these could inform your pedagogy and help you design evidence-informed projects for the students with whom you are working.

# 2 Developing a project-based learning culture

There is much unrest in education in the United Kingdom as I write this book, with debates coming from all sides as to what the purpose of education is and how children and young people should experience the process of learning. Whilst some argue that we need to return to more didactic methods of teaching, with children being monitored in each aspect of their school interactions, others are pushing forward to develop educational systems that encourage the innovative and creative skills needed for future employment. Our schooling experience was initially designed for a time when 36% of the working population were employed in manufacturing and 33% worked in service roles, such as domestic servants (Elliott, 2013). The Elementary Education Act of 1870 (UK Parliament, 2023) was a fundamental shift in the way in which education was shaped and required publicly funded schooling for all children in the United Kingdom between the ages of 5 and 13. Where parents could afford to pay, this was required, and it was compulsory for all children to attend school up until this age. The introduction of state inspections was implemented to confirm that high-quality learning was taking place in each setting, and we see this continuing across our educational systems in the United Kingdom. At the end of the year 2022, the proportion of those working in the manufacturing sector had decreased to 8% of the working population (Office of National Statistics, 2023), and job trends for the following ten years predict that technological roles will be in high demand as we move forward. There has also been a large increase in the number of people working in healthcare services, and for these roles, we have seen how technology is becoming integrated into care provision through the implementation of systems such as artificial intelligence, which can gather and predict trends or diagnose illnesses; blockchain technology, where information can be gathered, secured safely, and distributed across healthcare systems accordingly; and smart devices that can detect if an individual has fallen, remind people to take medication, and check factors such as blood pressure or sugar levels. Employees need new skills for their employment in this area and need to be able to make important decisions based on technological data. Paulo Freire (2017) outlines that there are two functions of educational systems in society. The first is to shape students to conformity, where they learn their position within societal hierarchies and how

DOI: 10.4324/9781003424345-3

to be compliant, and the second is to engage critically and reflexively within the society in which they live and learn how to make it better. Friere viewed this as the *Practice of Freedom*, an educational approach that can provide the students with whom we work with the skills to be change-makers and build our communities, structures, and mechanisms positively for the future. If our intention is to provide experiences for learning that nurture students' curiosity and create respectful dialogues where challenge is part of the learning process, we need to begin by reflecting on the role of the educator and how they are provided with trust and autonomy over their professional role. Whilst curricula are here to stay, we need to evaluate how we can create a culture within our schools and colleges that values each member of the teaching team and appreciates what their individual skills, knowledge, and interests can bring to our school life. A rigid, institutionalised structure as to how we teach as a whole will not prepare learners for economic prosperity, and we need to be aware that we are still drawing on a system that was created to keep everyone in their place and transition from school life to the factory floor. This is not to dismiss the value of those working within those roles; instead, it is to highlight that jobs such as these are reducing in number and students will require collaborative, critical thinking, and communication skills for future job roles.

The COVID-19 pandemic has also brought a shift to how we work. In the UK's Skills Gap Trend Report (The Skills Network, 2023), they report that the social media platform LinkedIn found that between March and May 2020, there was a 180% increase in job postings for remote working. Working from home is now here to stay, and this has opened up possibilities for more international connections and trade. It also requires individuals to be able to independently manage their time and responsibilities more frequently, and we will need employees who are able to embrace this way of working with confidence. Another trend highlighted in the report is the rise of jobs that support those with mental health conditions. A 230% increase in the demand for mental health-related skills across the last five years has been identified. This highlights a two-sided problem here. Firstly, we must recognise the impact of mental health conditions and develop infrastructure that adopts a preventative approach, and secondly, developing the skills in employees to support others in this area is of the utmost importance. Later in this chapter and throughout this book, I will consider further why educational settings need to focus more on the mental health of the staff team, but this statistic does remind us of the importance of adopting a holistic approach to supporting both staff and pupils and developing an environment where emotional responses are considered through both working and learning processes.

Of the ten soft skills required by employers in 2021, the highest required skill was communication, and the second was management (The Skills Network, 2023). Alongside these skills, there is also self-motivation, planning, and innovation. These trends and needs remind us again that educational systems need to be ones that develop individuals to be successful in future employment, and we have moved away from positions where people will largely move from education to manual labour. The skills of leadership, self-motivation, communication, and planning are all ones that are developed through the project-based learning experience, and we have a duty to provide young people with the skills to excel when they move on from schooling. The moral duty does not stop there. As we move into a new phase for employment opportunities, the recognition of the *Green Economy* is being globally discussed. In 2021, there was a 21% increase in job posts that required green skills (The Skills Network, 2023). Throughout this book, I discuss how we must take into account our connections and impact on the environment and the need to adopt a values-based approach when implementing project-based learning (PBL). Students are required, in project-based learning, to find solutions, and developing green skills will require us to look at situations from a new perspective compared to the industrial and mass production ages. We have progressed from the industrial and mass production revolutions, moving to a period where we require digital and technological advancements whilst balancing economic growth and preserving our planet. Connecting students to their local environment begins the journey of reflection and gaining an understanding of why we must protect what the world offers us as humans.

As our world continues to evolve with technological advancements and changing lifestyles, it is important, as educators, to prepare students with the skills required to feel confident in themselves as they progress. I am sure that any of us who experienced the lockdowns of 2020 will be able to reflect on how apparent this was as we moved to work from our homes and were still able to connect with the outside world. Now that experience has shaped how we move forward, artificial technology is at the forefront of discussions in education, and technology continues to develop further as we strive to keep up the pace of making sense of its impact and how to use technology effectively. As educators, we need to feel at ease with how our classrooms are extended through digital and technological resources and be empowered through professional development and dialogue with other educators to understand how these tools can enhance the learning experience. There are two main groups that will benefit from learning as changes continue to develop. The first is from the young people immersed in the technology and the second is from industry: Through project-based learning, we are able to concentrate on the right areas, listen to those using the tools, and consider further how and when they can be used and how we can facilitate a learning process that integrates these effectively.

All of this change requires us as educators to think about education differently and to stand firm to the values that guide us in our pedagogical approach. We need to consider in depth the reason and purpose of why we facilitate learning in the way that we do. If it is because it is how you are told to do it, the system says so, or it is because it is the way it has always been done, I would challenge you, with kindness, to pause and reflect on what has brought you to working within education. What is your 'Why?' How does your setting encourage you to follow this? Have you been proactive and shared it with the team with whom you work? A varied and creative approach to education provides both students and educators with a love for the learning environment and the ability to think critically about the purpose of each experience, developing it further as it progresses and keeping it relevant. Project-based learning is one key approach for embracing this mindset whilst also making it an enjoyable and stimulating journey for all.

**What leads our practice as educators?**

Twenge *et al.*'s (2010) research concludes that our motivations have changed across generations from *intrinsic* to *extrinsic* motivators. Intrinsic motivation is when we do something that provides an internal reward; we gain satisfaction from being engaged in a task rather than thinking about what the final outcome of it will be. Extrinsic motivation is when we focus on the outcome, seek a reward, or try to prevent ourselves from being punished for our actions. We are spending more of our time seeking to please others rather than focusing on the values and dreams that shape us. These motivations shape our behaviour, and with Twenge *et al.*'s (2010) research showing that young people are moving further towards more extrinsic goals, the current generation is eager to please others rather than feeling proud of themselves internally. We are living in a more materialistic and judgemental world, and these factors can be detrimental to our emotional health. We see it on social media: a focus on how many others hit the *like* button and the worry that comes from a small blemish being seen through the numerous filters added.

Extrinsic motivation prevents us from looking inward. We seek out approval and do things to please others. If I asked you, '*What is your purpose?*', how many of us could answer that without needing time to think it through? Project-based learning requires us to work as a team, but it also means we have to look within ourselves to consider our strengths and aspirations. That starts with us as educators in a position of influence. With a need to recognise emotional health in our day-to-day interactions, building our confidence and reflective skills will support us in approaching tasks holistically.

My days are frequently spent looking at new ideas and projects that I could be working towards. I see opportunities as I scroll online and want to do so many things. This requires an evaluative approach to how I look at my goals. I find myself reviewing three questions when embarking on something new: 'What will I gain from the experience?', 'Do I feel a need to find out more about the area that has left me curious?', 'Does this align with my goals, my values and my purpose?'. Let's explore this in a little more detail and consider what may motivate you as an educator when moving towards a project-based approach.

**What will I gain from the experience?**

Although financial gain is usually the driving factor and the fundamental reason for employment, it is not always the motivation needed to do something.

You may also find that, for the money offered, there is an imbalance between what you put in and what the payment will be. The extrinsic motivation of money might be what motivates you to sign up for something (and rightly so!) and there are very few of us in a position to turn down paid opportunities, but it is still something to consider before signing up for something. The opportunity may also provide you with the stepping stone you need for your career progression, another useful tool for determining if you should commit to something new. Reflecting on this area, you may find that you do want to progress to a higher level in the career you are in. You may also decide that you are currently content where you are. Both are valid, and this is why you need to stop and consider before jumping in with both feet. Then there is a purely intrinsic motivation: The project sparks your curiosity or will bring you joy. Every year I sign up for some projects that are work-related but provide no financial gain or that would support me in progressing up the career ladder. I do them purely because they are something that interests me and I know will hold my attention. They make me happy and contribute to me feeling satisfied with life. Sometimes it is my way of offering back what others have offered me during my early career. There are also times when friends and colleagues ask me if I would be interested in certain projects, and I know that I would not be putting my all into the project, so I politely decline. Thinking about our motivation and what will come from something is useful for understanding whether we want to embark on something new. It will be beneficial for us to think about our motivations when adopting project-based learning, as it supports in our consideration as to whether we feel we can embrace it and, in turn, provide students with the freedom and autonomy to lead learning experiences. PBL will push you out of your comfort zone; you will need to think more dynamically and feel comfortable with lessons changing course as students ask new questions and gain further knowledge that leaves them curious.

## Do I feel a need to find out more?

There are a lot of questions I want to explore, purely to find out how things work or why things happen. My son in particular has a way of asking questions as we progress through the day that makes me stop and think; it makes me pause what I am doing to explore something that has left me intrigued, as I do not know the answer. It is good to pause to explore that innate inquisitiveness, and it can bring many positive feelings when we do. However, there are also times when we do not need to find out more. Where we can feel satisfied that we know enough and know when to stop and move on to something that motivates us and brings us happiness. I am sure all of us can relate to a time when we spent too long on a task and lost interest. It was no longer satisfying and turned into a slog. This is when we need to make the decision that we do not need to find out more about a particular area. This can also be where teamwork can support us. If part of a task is becoming a slog and is no longer motivating, is it still purposeful? Do we need to evaluate and consider if it is still bringing purpose to others? Project-based learning can provide an avenue for you to remain curious and learn alongside students, maintaining relevance to the outside world whilst creating spaces for you to use creativity as an educator. The fact that you are reading this book should mean that you are curious about PBL and want to find out more, so you are already on your way to embracing project-based learning in your practice.

### Does the work align with my goals, values, and purpose?

Reviewing your purpose, goals, and values before you reach this step is important. My goals are continually evolving; for example, when I embarked on my lecturing career, I did not see writing as part of my professional journey, but it is now a large goal for me and my aspirations. This means that a lot of my goals are short-term, generally sitting around six months to three years, but they are clear and adaptable. Knowing my overall goal and keeping the smaller steps towards it clear and manageable means that I can give what I am working on my full attention.

Using Brene Brown's (2013) guide to exploring values, she encourages us to choose two that are most important to us. I have managed to get mine down to three, with two more that shape me (for anyone now interested, mine are kindness, play, and community. My two wider values are curiosity and nature). If a project does not align with these, I do not give it the green light to commence. I need to *feel* my progress and contribution, and by aligning my values with what I do, I know that feeds into my purpose. By going back to my values, I also know that if I commit to too much, then I am not being kind to myself or those with whom I am collaborating. Considering the time and commitment you can give is an important factor at this stage of your reflection. Starting your journey on PBL, reflecting on your professional values will support you in reflecting on how you will commit to a different approach (or evolve it further) with integrity, kindness, and purpose.

### Evaluating your commitment

Using a spiral reflection method may help you map out your or your students' decisions before embarking on a new project. When completing the evaluation, you may find that the project is not one you want to progress with as a collective, but it provides you with a reason why and develops the skill of critical thinking and an understanding of how to map curiosity to the curriculum and classroom experience. It will also support you in reflecting on whether you have the time, commitment, and resources to commence a project whilst providing a visual to share and discuss with others. The flow design is there to stimulate your creativity, and I would encourage you to add colour or doodles as you go, providing your mind with space to reflect as you progress in your evaluation.

*Figure 2.1* Spiral design created by the author Fey Cole.

## Developing a community space in the classroom

In Bell Hooks' (1994) book 'Teaching to Transgress', she stresses the importance of building communities within the classroom and for educators to critically review which voices are heard, ensuring that we recognise when one voice is the loudest and to make changes when this happens. Hooks (1994) focuses on the sense of community, where we recognise cultural codes, systems, or symbols that relate to a community of people. By recognising these codes, she describes this as a way for the educator to accept different ways of knowing and for educators to think more critically before they support the students they work with. With this approach to pedagogy and an awareness of multiculturalism embedded, Hooks (1994) concludes that this will create an environment that is values-based and prevents bias in our approach to practice. Begin your journey on project-based learning by critically reflecting on the resources and practice of your organisation, identifying where the tools and systems are led by the educator, and evaluating as a team how this can be developed to take into account the systems and experiences of the wider class community. With students leading learning experiences, our own biases and thought processes will be challenged, and we need to be open to embracing them rather than shutting them down as we do not see it as the *right* approach.

There are a number of other ways that you can develop a community space within the classroom that applies well to the project-based learning approach. Reflecting on the physical environment, goals- and curiosity-boards can be created, outlining both personal and collective goals for the group's time within the classroom. This needs to be an evolving and working feature where you come together to review it and evaluate progress at key points through the academic year. Goals may be removed and added, but it develops confidence in students to share ideas and feel as though they have ownership over their experiences.

Moving away from a conventional layout, with pupils facing towards the teacher, whilst also being able to move to different spaces within the classroom, will also support community building and build confidence within individuals to explore their learning in a way that works for them. I appreciate that we do not always have the physical space to move much around classrooms, but you may wish to consider a research area, a reading space, an exploration centre, and a group circle for people to come together to share ideas. Sitting side-by-side with pupils as an educator can make it much easier at times to listen intently to what they have to say and help you hear those quieter voices that can sometimes hide at the back.

Students' curiosities and research on their project-based learning goals will prompt bigger questions to which you, as an educator, may not have the answers. This is positive, as it shows that students' critical thinking and reflective skills are developing. This stage requires you to reflect on how you can facilitate and extend this further and consider the opportunities to connect with the wider community. In my book 'Intergenerational Practice in Schools and Settings' (Cole, 2022), I wrote about how frequently we segregate different age groups and how this impacts our mental health negatively whilst also missing out on a wealth of experiences and stories that can enhance our learning. Inviting people in to talk who have knowledge on a particular area or who are service-users of the topic you are exploring provides students with more clarity of the processes and a deeper connection to the area that is being researched. Project-based learning should encourage us to see that our classroom is more than the four walls that we find ourselves within, and planning trips and walks out in our community and meeting with our local businesses and organisations not only scaffolds our thinking but also develops that sense of belonging whilst making a difference through the end product of our project.

**Equal access**

An important aspect of equality is ensuring that equal thinking takes place. In Chapter 12, we explore in more detail the role of Nancy Kline's Thinking

Environment (1998) and how this provides a space for everyone to be heard. Project-based learning develops a culture where we evaluate in detail what is important to us whilst also looking outwards to the wider community and reflecting on what others value and need. This is not something that is often undertaken in traditional classroom experiences, and if the approach that is being used does not lend itself to all participants, then it is up to you as an educator to ensure that you have provided equal access for everyone involved. PBL lends itself to this easily, as it provides us with a mechanism to create a learning experience that suits everyone. You will be working in partnership with pupils, facilitating spaces that suit their needs, whilst the process encourages teamwork, where success comes from everybody achieving. This collaborative approach means that we have to think about other people and their experiences and contributions and not just ourselves, developing skills in the students that will enrich their future relationships whilst also looking at things from a different perspective.

## Social justice

Within education, we have a responsibility as educators to embed equality into all areas of our practice, and to do this, we must take into account social justice. Social justice education requires us to recognise inequalities that have previously been apparent, such as accessibility and opportunities being impacted due to level of family income, race, gender, and location, and challenge these moving forward. Dr. Crystal Belle (2019) promotes the importance of educators seeing students for who they are and encouraging the pupils we work with to question the world around them. A social justice approach to education is centred on democracy and recognises intersectionality so that we can respect the individuals in our classroom alongside the wider community – key requirements for project-based learning. Within a social justice framework, we should be encouraging students to look at things through the lens of others, taking into account multiple perspectives and acknowledging individuals for who they are, applying a person-centred approach.

Social justice in education is not new, and Dewey (Counts, 1932) wanted to create educational systems that made experiences more fair and just through democracy and that challenged inequitable social arrangements. This has continued to evolve as to how we approach educational systems now, and one way to consider how we create equitable learning environments can be seen through Hanesworth, Bracken and Elkington's (2019) approach to applying social justice within assessment processes. The universal learning design model (Hanesworth, Bracken and Elkington, 2019) draws on three principles that underpin how assessments are developed:

**Principle one:** This requires educators to reflect on how we as educators present information through multiple means of representation, recognising that we interpret information in different ways, and making sure there is a wealth of resources to present facts and content.

**Principle two:** This is probably the one that we may find most challenging as educators, as this requires us to differentiate the ways in which students can express themselves. How we express our ideas and learn moves away from the one-assessment-type approach, and students have autonomy over how they will present their learning.

**Principle three:** This is all about maintaining students' interest by providing multiple means of engagement. This can be done by understanding what challenges them and sparks their curiosity. Motivation for learning should be explored along with what students find exciting.

Adopting these principles can support you in developing assessment methods in PBL that are relevant and student-centred, valuing the individuals within the learning space, and, as an educator, there is something very exciting about seeing how students approach projects in a way that represents their ideas and concepts in a personal way. As you progress through your projects, listening and responding to students' voices is paramount. Consider your mechanisms for monitoring and evaluating how you are doing this, encouraging students to participate in your review meetings and discussions.

## Roles within the team

Collaboration is key for project-based learning, and the responsibility of projects should not fall upon the shoulders of a couple of individuals within the wider learning team. This is not just for students but also between students and educators and through the partnership of the teaching team. Recognition and awareness of the role of staff and students should be made clear, along with an understanding of how other stakeholders will support and enhance the projects you are working towards. Spend time developing 'roles and responsibilities checklists' that everyone agrees to and commits to, ensuring that everyone understands these and appreciates the part they play in the team.

## Developing a culture of collaboration and trust

Through training and role modelling collaboration amongst the staff team, trust will become embedded in procedures, and appreciation will encourage the team to try out their ideas to enhance the learning experience. The end product is important for project-based learning, but not as important as the process. The why and the how are something to be nurtured, and developing a culture where individuals can explore and have professional autonomy, whilst having mentors assigned to them with whom they can reflect will bring more creativity to the classroom and support a positive approach to working practices. We will return to this in more detail in Chapter 12, but removing the hierarchy within the educational system will provide much more confidence in the team's ability to embrace new projects whilst being nurtured in a way that ensures the projects align with the quality standards expected from the organisation.

## Reflective practice

Raelin (2002) suggests that in order for reflective learning to take place, it needs to be discussed and reflected on with others. From a constructivist approach, this allows individuals to give meaning to their learning. By sharing and becoming active in our learning (both for students and educators), we can fully understand the purpose of what we are doing. By sharing practice, we are able to discuss what we have achieved, areas we feel need further development, and opportunities for growth. Learning journals will be an important aspect of capturing the growth of understanding of skills and knowledge and should be undertaken by both students and educators, coming together to reflect on these as a wider group. Remember that journals do not just have to be recorded in a conventional written format. You may choose to do this through blogging, video entries, mentoring sessions, mind maps, or drawings. However the information is recorded, it is important to consider what happens following that reflection for further growth and development.

# 3 Growing as an educator through project-based learning

Early on in my career, I shifted from a career as a nursery nurse to a playworker. Through my qualifications, I was able to gain a managerial role but soon found challenges as I was not suitably trained in this specific area. I made the decision to go back to learning and began training as a playworker, and it quickly began to shape my leadership of play provision. I was working in a busy part of London, and many of the children required support with their self-regulation and emotional literacy. It was a tiring but satisfying role; we built strong relationships with the families we worked with, and seeing children relax into the environment and feel secure was a rewarding feeling as a professional. The children were mainly primary-aged, so they had progressed through play-based curriculums and playful experiences with their parents, but we found that many of the children did not know how to play. It was saddening that children were not able to explore their imaginations and found it difficult to concentrate on a task that did not have a clear objective. In my 22 years of practice, across different areas of the childcare sector, I have seen this frequently. Dr. Peter Gray (Mehta *et al.*, 2020) believes that play is a key evolutionary factor that we need as humans to succeed and survive in life, an inner impulse we all hold that directs how we learn. He focuses on three main drivers as to how we learn as mammals – play, curiosity, and sociability – but he voices a concern that it is easy for these to be dampened and even extinguished as we grow. Play is vital for learning, growth, and emotional well-being, so it is hugely beneficial for us to evaluate how we can develop learners' playful interactions to support them in engaging in activities. As we grow up, we frequently feel the need to suppress our play responses, and as children move into adolescence, it can be an embarrassment to be seen as engaging in play. It proves even more problematic to incorporate play into older classrooms when the individuals have grown up in environments with these limited opportunities to play in their childhood. In Mehta *et al.*'s interview (2020), Dr. Gray emphasises the role of the adult and the need for 'teachers to be trusted to teach', so how trusted do we feel to use play within the classroom?

I would encourage us to embrace play when incorporating project-based learning into our lessons. From our first meetings with students in the induction period, there is an opportunity to reflect on how we spark curiosity and build trusting relationships through our interactions. Short, project-based learning activities are a great way to do this, and strategies I have previously used have allowed for a shift from awkward icebreakers to sessions where everyone feels at ease to become involved. Here are three examples that you may wish to try in your own provision:

## Lego play

A nice task at the start of the year is to lay out the Lego bricks and encourage students to build models that represent the ideal team. For this task, I use a Padlet board with key questions included to encourage investigation and seeds of curiosity. This could also be easily produced with pens and paper on a noticeboard. Students are encouraged to speak with some of the stakeholders we work with, and previous students have recorded video blogs to provide examples of positive experiences of teamwork. This begins the initial research, with theories of teamwork reviewed by the class. The groups then work together to design their team with Lego, labelling bricks with certain values, attributes, and skills. The team ends this short project by sharing it with the other groups and creating a class manifesto of how we will support one another and our expectations for the year ahead. This proves a useful tool to return to throughout the year to see how we are developing as a team.

## Designing a newsletter

I spent a couple of years sending out a newsletter to students on different topics, such as upcoming events, projects we were working on, reading that would support them in their studies, and tips relevant to the work they were doing. It was well received, with students not only providing feedback informally about what they found useful about the newsletter but also providing me with feedback on what else they would find beneficial within it. I soon realised that this was something they could use as part of their own portfolio of evidence and also something they could share with wider stakeholders. Adopting the initial design as part of the induction process, students took responsibility for different sections of the newsletter that could be swapped throughout the year, and these pieces could be used as part of their assignments. The initial design focused on stakeholder questionnaires, including professionals, other students, teachers, and the students' parents. From these, artwork was created, and students considered how to design a newsletter that included artwork, imagery, and video links. By creating a bi-monthly edition from this, students were then able to build on their skills, create articles around their learning for others, and showcase other projects and events that they were working on.

## Spaces for downtime

How many of us arrive at school and work without lining our stomachs with breakfast and not getting the amount of rest that we should have had? I, for one, can hold my hands up here, and for others, this is something over which they have no choice. A good way to get to know students and understand how they study is to put them partially in charge of the timetable and to consider how rest and play are incorporated into the school week. Reviewing research on what makes positive learning environments and drawing on their own experiences, students can consider how to implement sessions or adapt lessons to ensure that downtime, which suits their needs, is incorporated. If it is a breakfast bar or social tea-time break, the students may wish to plan some events throughout the year to raise funds for this, and this could also incorporate showcasing some of the other projects that they are working on and inviting in others who can support them in research as part of a focus group. This planning around their learning space may also include some consideration for the layout of the classroom and the resources that are included. There may not be a budget for you to work from, but there could be collaboration with other classes and students that could enhance access to resources.

Through these activities, we are learning to trust our own intuition from the start of the academic year and are creating spaces that feel purposeful for both the students and ourselves. By developing spaces where pupils feel able to explore and lead sessions, we are creating an environment where we work in partnership within the classroom and draw on the pedagogy that shapes our teaching.

## Drawing on international practice

Part of my professional role is to support teachers who have not previously taught in the United Kingdom. It is a highly beneficial learning experience for me to gain an insight into how education is approached differently across continents, and although I am put in place as a mentor, the teachers provide me with new ideas and learning opportunities that strengthen my own practice. Whether we have been in the vocation for a long time, or it's our first day in the classroom, creating spaces for open dialogue in a trusting environment is a valuable tool where knowledge is exchanged across the team and sets the precedent for us to embrace creative thinking that develops into exciting lessons for the pupils.

We can find ourselves consumed by an insular view of how to approach education based on the curriculum and framework within which we work. Of course, this is largely due to us having to meet their expectations and the culture that surrounds us. However, it has brought much benefit to my approach to education to look outwards. Project-based learning is an approach frequently used across the globe, and even if we are unable to travel to observe this practice, we have the advantage of being able to connect with practitioners from around the world through social media and online events. Building a network through online platforms will bring new ideas for you to use in the classroom, and even if you see activities that challenge your thinking or that you do not agree with, reflecting on the reasons why will help you to craft your approach and return to the values that shape the way in which you teach. Working in a culture that shares and collaborates is a positive way to widen the experiences for the students you work with and acts as a reminder that we do not have to start projects from scratch, but instead, credit the individuals from whom you got the ideas and redesign them to suit the needs of the cohort that you are working with. Through connections such as this, I have sourced opportunities to work with others. In one project-based learning activity where we were researching with students how to design project-based learning activities within the early years, the UK student group connected with a group of students in Hong Kong. During this project, the students undertook research into the theories that underpinned this approach. This was a positive way to explore theory, and, thanks to technology, we were able to work on building our research projects across continents. Both student groups began to gain a wider perspective on approaches and recognise the similarities across our approaches, rather than focusing on seeing our educational systems as very different models. Widening the learning environment in this way can build the community around the student group and provide more people to learn from. The challenges that came to my own mindset also supported my growth as a professional and allowed students to see my learning journey, which is a great way to role model lifelong learning and build a space where questioning and curiosity are encouraged.

When talking to a colleague who works in Asia, we held a similar opinion about where project-based learning is most used, and this is often within schools that cost more to access and are classified as more aspirational. As an educator, I believe that a well-rounded and rich education system should not be for the chosen few and that systems need to be revamped for all to be able to access further economic and social experiences. Approaching education where all the emphasis is on final exam testing can decrease a student's intrinsic motivation to learn and lead to the attainment gap widening. Gardner, Holmes and Leitch (2019) describe examinations and tests not as something that supports learning but as, instead, something that categorises students, and they can be a tool that can further disadvantage those students who are already faced with barriers to education. Our responsibility as educators is to sometimes challenge the status quo. We will have to work within the restraints by which we are governed, but we can also approach lessons with the resources to inspire and provide students with full autonomy over their own learning experience. I do not think any of us enter the profession expecting to be rich financially by the end of our career, but we do have the opportunity to bring a richness to life that students will carry forward with them for a lifetime.

## Professional development

We can find ourselves rigidly working through professional development to ensure that we meet the regulated requirements and tick the box to confirm what we have completed. As role models for learning, we can find ourselves forgetting to do the crucial next step after completing the learning activity and undertaking a review of how it will support us in our practice. With professional learning sessions designed for us, we also find ourselves disengaged from the tasks, just like the students who are asked to undertake lessons where there is little autonomy. Lindsay (2016) discusses the history of mandatory continuing professional development (CPD) in the accounting sector and how it was used to quell the public's concerns regarding competency and, in doing so, means that individuals partaking in the activities are only passively educated rather than committing to life-long learning. This has started to be recognised across sectors, and there is awareness that CPD is not always a formal process. From this, there has been a range of evaluations in-house to identify the more informal learning that goes on within the professional role. Lindsay (2016) identifies that development needs to be continually evolving and responsive to an environment of change, with the individual using reflexivity as a critical skill in their learning. The informal learning process is just as significant as the formal one and acts as a reminder that reflecting on a range of professional development activities can support us in developing our skills throughout our careers. Within Chapter 12, you will be introduced to the *Alexandrite EDPRO* framework, which explores professional learning in more detail and is a great way to evaluate the effectiveness of our teaching. Activities such as action research are a positive addition to those implementing project-based learning, as they require a review of what the outcome of practice is.

Alongside our more formalised professional learning, we also should value the impact of collaborative exchanges between professionals, reading relevant books and articles, and getting out to visit other settings and organisations that relate to our vocational and subject areas. Re-entering your classroom following a job shadow with someone who is directly using their educational subject for their role can stimulate a lot of excitement and relevance as to why students are learning particular outcomes. Consider how you will plan your annual journey to take informal learning into account and use each activity to evaluate how it will enhance practice moving forward. The following table may support you in doing this and reflecting on the benefits it brings to both you and your students:

## Professional learning evaluation

Personal reflection (purpose of the learning, intended learning goals, how it supports me in my professional journey, what the expected outcomes will be)

When using the learning within the classroom, I found that:

From this learning, I have now been able to:

The key research and theoretical approaches that underpinned this learning were:

I now need to (consider your next steps):

When sharing this with colleagues, I learned that:

I have changed my thinking through this learning because:

This learning will bring change through:

The gaps in my learning in this area since this activity are:

This learning has linked to the following other learning activities that I have completed:

My final reflection:

## Reflection

As educators, we sit in a privileged position and must consider how we adopt a value-based and ethical approach to all that we do. Our words and actions influence others, and it is important that we pause and reflect on the information that we present and share with others. At the time of writing this book, there were big discussions on what leadership should look like and questions as to whether decisions made by those in power had been acceptable ones. The innovation and advancement of industrial and technological resources and trades lead us to a point where we must consider not just the positive benefits that they bring but also how they impact us negatively. Our natural world requires care, and the divide between rich and poor in western society is becoming wider. How we lead needs to be an area of consideration as we progress forward; it brings no benefit to society when only a privileged few gain rewards. Education provides us with a pathway for young people to learn the importance of thinking about the wider community rather than only working towards goals that bring gain to one individual. There is space for different approaches to education, but remaining with a system where students are expected to sit up, shut up, and listen is far from where we need students to be if we hope to provide them with the skills to be critical-thinking leaders who can break the cycle of only the selected few reaching positions of change-making. The way we live our lives at the moment in the West is not sustainable. Change is needed, and it will be up to our young people to bring this. We cannot disempower them by only providing them with learning experiences where others think on their behalf. Moving forward, all leadership skills should be underpinned with sustainability knowledge with the ability for pupils to not just consider their work with people in mind but also in relation to the natural world. When designing your projects with students, I would highly encourage you to evaluate how these skills are developed so that young people can bring them forward into their working and later social lives.

# 4 Developing spaces that embrace flow and curiosity for learning

I live in a beautiful part of the world, and Northern Ireland's landscape is very green, with much of our land allocated for farming. I was once on a plane, flying back from London, when I heard a loud 'WOW' from the row behind me. A man from America enthusiastically shared his excitement of seeing somewhere with such a different landscape from what he was used to, and he told the surrounding passengers that he had never seen somewhere so green. Everything looked green, he told us! The joy we all shared from his excitement brought a warm and proud feeling for those of us that were residents of the Emerald Isle, alongside the slightly miserable awareness that we gain a lot of that green from the vast amount of rain that falls! We did not burst his bubble and share how frequently the clouds showered us, but I am pretty sure we were all in agreement of this fact and that he would soon find this out for himself after being in the country for a few days!

We do get a lot of rain, but our country is very much tailored for being outdoors. As soon as the sun shows its bright light in the sky, many of us head for a walk or out to the garden. Our wardrobes include the many layers needed for the frequent four seasons that we find in one day. One of our local parks spends much of the time in the winter with rain-flooded paths, and this is one of my favourite walks. My son and I have a habit of taking our shoes off and rolling up our trousers to continue on our journey, and that certainly provides me with laughter and happiness that clears any troubles from my head. During the winter months, my family and I head to the North Coast of Northern Ireland, and no matter how cold it is, you will find us jumping the waves alongside the surfers and more professional swimmers. We have a hardy culture here when it comes to the cold and storms!

When working on some collaborative projects with educators from Asia, I had to think differently about how the climate can impact using the outdoors for learning when developing sessions for international educators, and I worked closely with colleagues in Spain and Hong Kong to review the differences that the weather brought to how we could use the outdoors as a learning space. At a conference recently, I listened intently to a speaker from India who explained that due to the air quality, there were times each day that could not be spent outside as the pollution would impact negatively on individuals'

DOI: 10.4324/9781003424345-5

health if too much time was spent outdoors. We have a lot to learn as humans as to how to look after our planet, ensure that we protect it, and spend time on it to remind ourselves of what a crucial necessity it is for us all. In whatever part of the globe you live, I would encourage you to evaluate how you can use outdoor spaces to develop mindful spaces that give you the capacity to move and be free to explore curiosity. When I find myself sitting at a desk too long to work, I know I need to move, and getting outside often brings me the change I need to get my brain active again, finding new ways to approach work and gaining fresh ideas to bring back to the task at hand.

**Biophilia and classroom design**

As already noted in this chapter, we are not always able to get outside to learn. I wish we could, and I will keep pushing for it wherever I can, but the reality is that for the majority of us, a large proportion of the day will be spent in the classroom. This is where biophilia comes into play. Biophilia recognises that humans have an innate connection to nature, both physically and emotionally. By using biophilic design in our classrooms, we consider how the built environment can incorporate nature and bring the outdoors in, complementing the two worlds we find ourselves connected to.

The first step in designing our biophilic space is to consider the colour scheme within our classroom. We often find ourselves in classrooms with garish primary colours when working with children in their younger years, before moving to bright whites with fluorescent lighting for older pupils. Adopting a biophilic approach, we alternate the colours to those of the earth, such as a natural green, sea blue, or a warm, earthy brown. Research undertaken in the Netherlands found that, within a study with 170 pupils, children working in a classroom with a green wall had higher scores on selected activities than their peers in a classroom without one (Van den Berg *et al.*, 2017). Taking the colour and natural theme further, you could consider the introduction of a living wall, a wall where plants grow naturally from a vertical frame. During the lockdown period of 2020, when most individuals across the globe were restricted to staying at home, a research study was undertaken by the UK Centre for Ecology and Hydrology (Pocock *et al.*, 2023) to evaluate the impact that spending time with nature had on well-being and happiness. Five hundred participants carried out ten-minute nature-based activities at least five times over an eight-day period. Activities included citizen science projects such as environmental monitoring as well as nature-noticing activities that included sitting in a green space and writing down three positive things that they observed. All participants reported a greater connection to nature following the experiment and higher levels of well-being. Connecting with nature does not require a huge amount of space; a small area, such as a living wall, can provide students with a project for them to create and connect with. An hour spent each week on the space could explore design and implementation, edible plants to use in cooking, water systems for the plants to thrive, engineering processes, materials, patterns, and many different mathematical and scientific research questions that the pupils decide to investigate. If a wall is not possible for your space, an inside growing space can be just as effective if students take ownership of its development. The Mental Health Foundation (2021) reports that connection with nature is more impactful for making a positive difference to our mental health than just spending time with it. It has also been found that this stronger connection leads to us being more proactive in pro-environmental activities, an important area that we should be promoting within the classroom throughout project-based learning (PBL) activities. Creating high-quality nature spaces both indoors and outdoors leads to better environments both physically and mentally, which are important areas to focus on when wanting to create learning spaces for individuals to thrive academically.

Tidball (2012) identifies two components of biophilia. The first is that, as humans, we have an affinity for other living things, and this is rooted in our biology. As our lived environments take us further away from the natural world so frequently, we find ourselves spending less and less time with the natural world. Time spent at desks with limited access to the natural world leads to mental fatigue and our diminishing concentration levels. Reflecting on the sensory experience within your classroom can help you to consider how you can design it with neurodiversity in mind and help to create spaces of calm for all those who use the area. Moving concentration spaces so that they are lit with natural light, using appropriate aromas, and adding displays that flow in their design can all help to maintain engagement and encourage creativity.

## Learning outdoors

Spending time outside is often seen as play time within western educational systems and can be undervalued. Over the past few years, I have been fortunate to have a space dedicated to outdoor learning and use this frequently instead of our brick-built classroom. Using action research, I wanted to see the impact spending time outdoors had on students, and for the space of a term, students rated on a scale of one to ten how they felt at the end of lessons both indoors and outdoors. I was shocked by the difference between the two, and students jumped as many as four or five points in the questionnaire in feeling more confident in their ability, having a greater focus on the tasks, and feeling able to fully complete the activities following time spent in the outdoor environment. The expectation of sitting in a room for six hours a day is not one that we should strive towards, and having the freedom to move lessons from indoors to outside can support students in being inspired by the natural world and having a clearer head when concentration is needed.

The use of learning walks can be very beneficial for collaborative tasks, building professional relationships with pupils, and mentoring activities. Moving tutorials from inside to a walking session can help to put individuals at ease and make them feel more comfortable sharing any tricky situations they may find with their work. It can also be less intimidating. Being able to walk side-by-side rather than looking directly at the individual can help pupils feel able to share worries or concerns they have. The formalities of the classroom disappear, and the power imbalance can be removed from the teacher-student dynamic. The same can be said for conversations with peers. A walk, where particular points of consideration to discuss are presented by the educator, can form an engaging conversation amongst peers that can be further developed once back together in one space.

As an early years educator, outdoor learning has always been highly important to me. In my job role, I not only get to share my vocation with others, but I also get an insight into different areas of education. My own approach to further education encompasses play, curiosity, and movement, often found in the early years, but I have adapted this to encourage students to find flow and focus during their studies whilst embracing these different areas. Throughout 2020–2021, the importance of connecting to nature and the stimulation it brought to learning seemed more apparent than ever. As someone who likes to explore, we spent many days prior to the COVID-19 lockdown periods out on visits and walks, and this contributed to the findings as part of my own action research. Like many of the team, we found ourselves connecting much more with students during the period of lockdown, and it gave us the opportunity for informal conversations that made our relationships stronger. The introduction of walking tutorials prior to the pandemic, where students paired up with each other or myself to work through their plans, was something that we felt we did not want to lose and was adapted to suit the shift to being physically apart during lessons. During this period, walks were still essential to our schedule and broke up our online lessons. Sharing our ideas from walks and photographs of where we had found inspiration allowed us to continue to work collaboratively and was an essential part of how PBL continued. Following this period, we now see teams adopting hybrid working models and more flexibility as to where they work. Using different spaces and environments to work and learn in will be essential in future employment, and students need to be able to transition to still working in connection with teams whilst physically being apart from them. Promoting the importance of utilising outdoor spaces will support individuals' mental health whilst also teaching adaptable skills.

My research on outdoor learning got me thinking about how we frame things and how we have a choice as to whether we do this positively or negatively. So often we hear the phrase 'the calm before the storm'. We approach things with an air of caution, waiting for bad things to happen and trying to prevent things from getting *messy*. I want to reframe this so that we embrace the puddles, the messiness, and the play. So instead of the calm before the storm, how about we instead see it as the 'rain before the rainbow?' How will you embrace the messy that sparks curiosity and moves from static learning to bringing colour and imagination into what we do?

### Removing power imbalance within the classroom

When reviewing your teaching space, it is a helpful activity to sit in the spaces where learners will be. If you are able to sit in the space when someone else is teaching and participate in the lesson, this is even better. Developing a culture of non-competitiveness and removing judgement from these types of activities makes it much easier for you to develop these opportunities to share one another's environments. When sitting in the student's chair, you will gain a deeper appreciation of how easy it is to participate and any physical barriers there may be. In a typical classroom from the primary years up, the teacher will be at the front of the room, with the students directed towards them. This in itself can create a power imbalance between educator/pupil and can often lead to only the more confident students, or the students at the front, contributing to discussion. I have frequently moved furniture around mid-lesson as I can feel this barrier to connection, and often sitting in a circular shape alongside students can break down that barrier to participation. Participating in activities alongside students and trying out the classroom exercises can help students understand the process much better. It also helps you to understand the barriers that may come about; for example, if you are using a new online quiz platform, you will gain awareness of any complications that may come from logging on and participating. Seeing the classroom through the eyes of the student is important to ensure that what we do together is effective for all participants.

**The theory of flow**

Whilst writing this book, I moved spaces due to a change in job role. Any change, even when positive, can bring a little unease, and I recognised that I was finding it challenging to feel like myself in the new space. I took a little step back to reflect and consider what was contributing to this feeling, returning to my studies of Mihaly Csikszentmihalyi's theory of flow. Csikszentmihalyi (1990) discussed the importance of creating spaces that reflect our identity through symbols. Csikszentmihalyi said that those who spend more time in beautiful surroundings see situations more holistically, and whether we are working from home, the office, or from the car, time should be spent displaying symbolic items that we feel drawn to. For me, I instantly started to relax in my new space once I had some pebbles from the seaside on my desk, some items that represented my professional role, and some other little trinkets that had memories attached. Reviewing our practice and the surroundings we work in is important to approach holistically if we want to truly grow within our roles.

Throughout Csikszentmihalyi's research (1990), he suggests that when we are engaged in a challenging situation whilst learning, we can become happier. We want to find ourselves in activities where other things do not matter, as we are absorbed in the moment. We continue to do things for the sake of it and do not be disrupted by the many stimulants we find ourselves distracted by in this modern era. Project-based learning (PBL) should include many periods when we can participate in an uninterrupted flow. Being able to be flexible in lessons where activities can be extended and evolve through the interactions of students is an important aspect of making your projects a serious element of classroom learning.

Csikszentmihalyi (1990) says that our minds will lean towards the negative when we are idle. Negative experiences can impact more greatly on decision-making, not focusing enough on positive or neutral views. This would have been useful for humans when we lived as hunter-gatherers, looking out for the warning signs of an attack from a hunting creature, but it is not so useful nowadays that it leaves us in a state of fight or flight in the office. Termed negativity bias, it is important for us to recognise the impact of this on how we approach decisions and review both the positive and negative to choose a path that adopts a balanced reasoning and approach. Being busy does not have to be loud; quiet engagement with tasks will aid the development of projects, and we can continue to review how we consider mental health holistically with learning opportunities.

To be in a place of flow, Csikszentmihalyi (1990) says that clear goals should be in place. Aware that stress is a normal part of people's lives, he did not feel that these are factors that we need to actively remove but instead are something that does not disturb us when we are focused on an activity. Flow allows us to be at our most creative and creates a space in our mind where we are absorbed in the situation that we find ourselves in. When working with students, I have seen them engaged in flow, where they continue to work on a project after the lesson has ended, determined to complete the element they are completing and doing this using creative methods. Work should not hinder other aspects of our lives, but when we find happiness in activities, it is great to see this concentration take place. It is a good feeling as an educator to see students wanting to work past their lesson time rather than wanting to rush off as soon as it is over!

In Walker's (2010) study, consideration was given to whether flow is better in a group or independently. The research showed that students found flow more enjoyable when with others, and this increased when the students were able to talk with one another. PBL needs to be done as a collaborative activity. We have seen in Chapter 1 how collaboration aids academic development, but we also see how working with others can help us find joy in what we do. It has been calculated that on average, **90,000** hours of our lives are spent at work (Gettysburg College, 2023); we need to find happiness within that time and ensure that we find work where we can that leaves us feeling fulfilled.

**Embracing play for learning**

When my son was around 11, he returned from some playtime with his friends out in the local village and told me that there had been a strict referee for the group's football match. The referee had kept them in check with their behaviour, disallowed a couple of goals, and my son seemed satisfied that the game had been fairly managed, even if there was a little whinging about this fairness in the game! I was left a little perplexed; he had been over on the play fields, I thought, and I wondered if I was confused and if he had instead been over with the football coaches at our local club (another frequent play spot for the group). I was not confused; they had been out on the fields, and it turns out that their game was followed professionally, with one of the children preferring to be in the role of referee to being one of the football players. The individual was clearly respected by my son, and it made me think about how we can naturally find ways to best utilise our skills and expertise from a young age. Although football is a structured game that the group is well used to playing, each individual chose to do something they enjoyed. Different positions and responsibilities were agreed upon, and they spent the time participating in something they wanted to do. When we begin to agree on team positions as part of PBL, it can be useful to leave people to play for a while so that they can find their natural position. When left with the resources and prompts for the project, we need to step back as educators after encouraging students to consider where their skill set lies within the activity.

Before moving into a large PBL activity, it can be beneficial to incorporate play into sessions for people to feel confident in putting forward ideas and feel less pressure if things do not work out the way that was expected. Play is an inmate and biological need that we need to embed more into learning experiences. Dictating what role individuals will play can leave individuals disengaged and with a lack of interest in participating. There may be times when encouragement to try out different roles is important. We should not see the same person as the project manager in all the projects we do, but when values of listening and playfulness are embedded, pupils should find themselves wanting their peers to try out different positions and do what enables them to thrive. Play provides us with a mechanism for testing out roles and learning about what we are good at in a safe space.

During the process of writing this book, I took a trip to New York with my best friend. Whilst out exploring, we had a walk along Fifth Avenue, and as my friend went off to buy something, I took the opportunity to rest for ten minutes on a couch within one of the stores. I could not help but listen when I noticed the shop's staff team using a playful focus to approach their team meeting. Each section's leader had designed a play activity to test the team's knowledge in a particular area. A quiz took place by someone who was new to leading this, and individuals responded as quickly as they could to questions asked to win their section points. When a question was answered incorrectly, kind laughter and the correct answer were provided, and it was evident of the positive teamwork characteristics of the group. The playful approach to making sure that everyone knew what they needed to was done with ease and connection, and it reminded me how play looks differently across age groups but is an important and essential behaviour for us all to use for learning and growth.

## Creating knowledge spaces

We will learn more about Nonaka (Helgesen, 2008) in Chapter 5, but his theory proposes that organisations need to become better at creating knowledge, and through the use of *Ba*, people are encouraged to set time aside to discuss and gain a deeper understanding of each other. Having time for groups to get to know one another and care for each other develops a trusting community for us to learn in and opens the opportunity for students to feel secure in sharing their learning. Brainstorming and active listening activities can help students think through how to move their project to the next level and extend their thinking further.

The concept of *learning as becoming* describes how this is 'a way of talking about how learning changes who we are and creates personal histories of becoming in the context of our communities' (Lindsay, 2016). As students learn how to think critically and evaluate their learning, they should be evaluating how this knowledge relates to their professional identity and how it relates to their later vocational role. As educators, we want students to see past the restraints of the four walls of the classroom and believe in their own abilities as they move forward. Contextualising knowledge to show how it relates to individual pupils broadens the experience and draws on the collective values of all participants.

**Messy learning**

The title of this chapter may have led you to think of unmanaged and unorganised spaces, but that is not what messy learning is. Messy learning is about thinking critically and creating an environment where everyone can be themselves and engage creatively. Rigid learning, where a teacher dictates what the students learn, does not encourage the skills for developing pupils into lifelong learners and is not going to be effective for PBL. Having the flexibility for students to move from their seats, take inspiration from the world around them, and connect with one another can open up a world of possibility.

# 5 Scaffolding learning through project-based learning

Project-based learning (PBL) is a great way for pupils to follow their own interests through intrinsic motivation. Differentiation within the lesson supports deeper investigation, and students are able to see their individual progression. When we are interested in something, the likelihood is that we will challenge ourselves further. This can be seen as students become more confident in following their interests and feel more autonomous over the situation. PBL requires students to find information from a variety of resources and moves away from being directed by the teacher. As students develop their research skills, the accessibility of information becomes much broader through PBL, and they can find the tools that work most effectively for them. Enriching the resources and exploring new ways to gather information is a positive way to learn together and encourage choice in the approach students will take to their projects. Whether students use books or weblinks or get out into the community to talk to others, there are a range of possibilities that can deepen students' understanding of a topic, providing them with mechanisms for making sense of the information that they find. Maintaining a journal log of what has been read and how it has impacted the student is one way to promote engagement in reading and research whilst working through projects.

Throughout this book, I hope it is evident how projects can evolve and develop. Although an end point for projects is important, we need to be able to reflect in the moment and consider how we can increase the opportunities and scaffold learning throughout the project journey. Evaluating how we work with others, considering our environment and resources, and adapting as we go are important elements for increasing our learning capacity throughout each project.

## Space and place

In the last chapter, we explored the importance of getting outside of the classroom when engaged in PBL. When putting together plans for an outdoor learning space, interwoven into this was the theory of *Ba* (Nonaka and Konno, 1998), a concept from the Japanese philosopher Kitaro Nishida. *Ba*, loosely translated in the English language to 'place', recognises the interconnectedness between person and place and considers how spaces can be used for knowledge creation. It is seen that within shared spaces, we are able to understand the knowledge and experiences of others whilst in turn sharing our own perspectives and turning information into fresh ideas. This brings recognition of our own limitations and the opportunity to open up to creative ways of thinking with others. This theory not only led to understanding how outdoor spaces were an environment that provided us with a foundation for knowledge creation but also resonated with informal spaces that we use day-to-day with students. This included virtual spaces that needed to be recognised as just as important to the spiral of learning that we were travelling through on our journey through the academic year. It was important to blend our connections with nature and our 21st-century skill set for students to be able to flow through the projects that they are working on.

*Ba* theory (Nonaka and Konno, 1998) allows us to focus on a particular time and place, which is important for us as we build on our learning and approach our studies through relevant projects that relate to students' experiences and the social action approach we adopt throughout our courses. Responding to the natural world and what was taking place around us linked to one of our underpinning values, 'curiosity'. A values-based approach was critical for students to feel safe and secure in exploring their ideas and concepts, and it supported them in feeling confident to lead our learning rather than teachers setting out each week's agenda. It is easy to fall into the habit of teaching the same material each year, but as a team, we saw it as vitally important that teaching be relevant to the students' own journeys and provide space for knowledge to be scaffolded further. This strategy did not lead to extra work for teachers because students took ownership of their ideas and came up with the plans for our approach. It is a refreshing process that keeps the joy in our shared experiences between teachers and students.

From the theory of *Ba* came the development of the SECI model (Nonaka and Takeuchi, 1996). Nonaka and Takeuchi evaluated the concepts of explicit and tacit knowledge, concluding that Western culture often focuses too much on explicit knowledge rather than the tacit knowledge that is formed around our values, emotions, and individual experiences. The model blends the different types of knowledge and the process of knowledge creation through four key steps.

Within the SECI model, a 'knowledge creation spiral' sees knowledge continually created and transformed as those involved in the process build on their learning, collaborate with others, and engage with the process. This framework has worked well for us as it complements the approach we were aiming for to make learning exciting and student-focused. Our recognition of how knowledge is created, with an understanding of the value of space, has led to a collective strength in appreciating our own abilities and also committing further to life-long learning. There is still a lot of growth as progression continues if we embrace the spiral of learning. Recognising that shifts will depend on individual aspirations and external factors will influence our thinking.

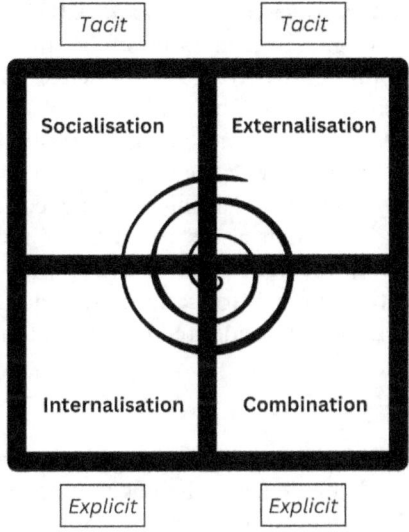

*Figure 5.1* SECI model. Image created by the author.

## Creative curriculums

Following World War II, Loris Malaguzzi (Edwards, Gandini and Forman, 2012) created educational environments built on values within communities united in wanting a positive change in their society. Caroline Pratt (2014) developed innovative project-based, play-led teaching methods after recognising the repression of formal education. A creative approach to education is a powerful tool following suppressive periods and acts as a positive catalyst for creating spaces for students to become critical thinkers who are committed to personal and societal growth. Adopting a holistic approach to learning where we value each individual's contribution and ideas helps us consider how we implement experiences where the whole group is able to thrive. One fundamental skill that can often get lost in curriculums is *learning how to learn*. The rushed requirement to get through the content covered in curriculums can widen the gap for students who find it challenging to understand the building blocks to get to the next stage. Students will quickly switch off. Thinking of my own experiences in education, I did so myself with a subject I found challenging. It did not take long to be left behind, and I believe I did not have the capacity to achieve the requirements. Returning to the subject some years later, I could feel my invisible armour clunking around me and a resistance to stepping back into the classroom. It is not surprising that students switch off when they are not taught the purpose of learning and how to do it. The pressure on teachers to focus on results rather than students is something that needs to be tackled at both team and policy-maker levels. Taking a step back and reviewing how we do this with those who are disengaged will be a positive aspect of implementing PBL into your programme of delivery.

Research undertaken in America (Duke et al., 2021) found that students who used PBL had a 63% gain in their social studies in contrast to their peers in the comparison group. This percentage translated to five to six months of increased learning for the year. The study took place in a setting located in a high-poverty area, and it was noted that typically PBL is used within schools where families are on a high income. Implementing activities where students had autonomy over their learning not only led to the students gaining increased learning, but results also showed a 23% increase for the group for informational reading: the equivalent of two months of learning for the year. Using an authentic approach to learning, we adopted equitable values and evidenced why PBL should be adopted for all children and young people.

**The importance of play**

In Mainland China, the Ministry of Education prohibits kindergarten settings from implementing academic lessons, such as writing or arithmetic (Li and Rao, 2005). Although academic focus comes in later years, there is an understanding of the value of play and how it supports children's development. The use of eduplay in Chinese pre-school settings is the adoption of play-based learning that includes Chinese characteristics. Whilst I was researching different approaches across Europe and Asia, I was introduced to AnjiPlay during a session at the International Play Association Conference. Hearing about the values and methodology reminded me of how essential play is for children's holistic growth, and it was wonderful to hear about the philosophy behind the early years' educational approach. Based on five principles – love, risk, joy, engagement, and reflection – Ms. Cheng Xueqin (Anji Education, 2023a) has designed an approach in the county of Anji that encourages children to participate in uninterrupted purposeful play. The programme has been recognised by China's Ministry of Education and adopts *true play* experiences, where children have freedom to explore the materials and environment that have been facilitated by the educators. Implementing this approach was not without its challenges, and parents were not content when the method was initially trialled (Anji Education, 2023b). Parents and grandparents were invited in to observe sessions and shift their perspective on the benefits of their children engaging in true play, with many of those parents going on to train later parents on the observation and documentation activities. I was inspired when listening to the session and the shift that had been brought about: AnjiPlay is an approach I would encourage any early years' educator to learn more about, and it is now gaining traction in other continents. The five interconnected principles are ones that all of us in education should consider adopting when implementing learning activities for the pupils with whom we are working. The impact of true play environments also shows how impactful play can be for learning and should encourage us to review how we can use play to scaffold learning.

As a Further and Higher Education lecturer, I place just as much value on play with adult learners as I do with young children. Play is not something that only little ones engage in; it shifts as we move through the years. Playing with technological gadgets and apps to try something new, recording our work through videos and artwork, using Lego to represent our ideas, and designing a team quiz are all examples of ways that we can engage with play and build on our learning whilst engaging in PBL.

**Scaffolding learning further**

For us to scaffold learning effectively as educators, we need to know students and be aware of their individual knowledge and skills. The way in which you design the framework of your projects should consider the age and stage of the group and how experienced they are at taking ownership of their own learning. In Chapter 12, we look in more detail at how to use particular activities to support PBL, but considering how we facilitate space for growth to be explored is important throughout the whole journey of implementing PBL experiences. When facilitating PBL, we need to differentiate the ways in which knowledge and skills are shared so that everyone is supported effectively, and when students can speak in a trusting and open environment, they will be more able to understand what approach is effective for them. Role modelling – how we think through points of curiosity and use spaces for students to debate and question – will help build the skills of critical thinking and reflection.

In 1962, American President John F. Kennedy visited the NASA mission control centre, and whilst he was on tour around the building, he stopped to talk to one of the janitors. Asking the janitor about what he did at the centre, the man replied that 'he was helping to put a man on the moon' (Nemo, 2014). When we work within a team, we do well to recognise and appreciate the role that each of us plays. Within PBL, outlining the different roles and responsibilities of each team member strengthens the collaborative achievements and also makes it clear what each participant needs to do to reach the collective end goal. Providing a clear insight into what the group is working towards develops a purpose and vision that everybody is striving towards and builds respect amongst peers. Everyone needs to lead an element; roles may shift as different projects progress, but most importantly, everyone is valued, and learning builds for each participant.

# 6 Overcoming barriers when implementing project-based learning

There may be significant barriers that can prevent us from embarking on the project approach, and this chapter will review some of these in further detail to consider how we overcome them whilst building the confidence of both the teaching team and the students. In many educational approaches, we are used to the educator taking the lead, and it can be daunting to shift the direction so the students are in control of what comes next. It can also be intimidating when faced with barriers, and a lack of confidence can lead to us abandoning the approach and feeling the need to return to more traditional classroom teaching. Recognising the barriers and having an awareness of how other educators have responded to them can support us in developing strong and purposeful projects that will meet stakeholder and organisational expectations. The length of this chapter is not to put you off! Instead, it is to review these barriers in detail whilst evaluating how they can be overcome.

## Authenticity

Authenticity needs to be our starting point with any project. To spark pupils' creativity, they need to see the purpose of what they do. I am someone who switches off very quickly if I am unable to see the value of what I am doing. In life, sometimes we do have to do tasks such as this, but it is also important that joy be found in the activities that we undertake. We have to adapt our projects depending on the group we are working with and the individuals within it.

Anne Reardon-James, a Further Education Practitioner from Wales, stresses the importance of projects being meaningful and the importance of educators taking time to consider how projects are relevant to all learners, preventing the risk of individuals taking on all the responsibilities. By reflecting on these areas from the outset, we can consider how we will engage all individuals and ensure that everyone knows and understands their role. Students need to be involved from the planning stage and will help you agree on what your motivations will be moving forward.

DOI: 10.4324/9781003424345-7

## Lack of connections

Finding real-life examples to draw on with students requires us to make connections with our wider community. There are many reasons why this may prove problematic, and finding time to source external support can sometimes prove near-impossible when reviewing the calendar. In my own role in vocational education, this has been much easier than it might be when working within other educational levels, as we frequently meet with professionals to organise students' placement experiences. It can take time to connect with people outside of our settings, and it will require stepping outside of our usual routine to do so. Getting outdoors can be the first step to building on these connections, and it can be useful to consider who can come in to speak with your pupils from the local community. Building any links with local organisations and businesses can create a stronger society and open up more opportunities. It is not all down to you as the educator to source these links, and it can be useful to encourage students to consider how they make these links themselves. Making calls and writing letters and emails can develop skills that the students you work with will require in the future, and, from experience, many students now find it daunting to phone someone they do not know to make inquiries. Preparing for this and building confidence through role-play will make it much easier for them when they move out to the workplace. For younger children, letters could be submitted with support, drawings included with their inquiries and an additional note from you as the educator to explain in more detail what the child is investigating. We need to encourage the confidence young people have to inquire and question, not dampen it and expect adults to do all the talking on their behalf.

Whilst working on an intergenerational project, students were planning to go on learning walks with older residents from the community to explore how the town has changed between generations and what we could put in place to develop spaces in the town that could be used to bring people together and tackle social isolation. Whilst planning this project, we realised that if you were to do a walk of the town, there were not many sitting spaces for individuals to rest, an important factor for those with limited mobility who were unable to participate in the walk without rest. This led to us evaluating social spaces from a new perspective and developing sitting spaces we could use in identified areas of the town. We also collaborated with the local council, and representatives attended one of our get-togethers, to undertake a feedback consultation session. Since this time, the council now has 'chatty benches' located around the town where people are encouraged to take a rest and talk to anyone that they find themselves sharing the bench with. The benches were not our project, but the collaborative approach of different organisations led to a focus on the need for connection and new spaces for this within the community, and it is lovely to see people using these spaces whilst we are on our travels. The learning outcomes that we were working towards were still covered, and we also made a positive impact on our local area.

Our curiosity can be sparked in a variety of ways, and utilising the local, natural environment is another way to find new connections. Your project may come from your connections to nature. When taking a walk in the park, pupils may recognise that the water levels in the local pond are lower than they were the week before; they may notice that there are particular areas in the town where rubbish is frequently dumped; or it could be observed that the blossom is budding earlier than it should be. Considering these three observations, there are a variety of reasons why this might happen, and there are problems in these discussions that could lead to a wider project that incorporates a range of subject areas. We need to be able to connect with the physical space around us, and when we incorporate projects that focus on areas such as this, it also develops an ownership of spaces where more care and consideration are given to how we look after the natural world.

We need to be engaged with our local environment. It forms part of our culture and identity, and when we feel disconnected from it, it can lead to a variety of negative responses. Do students tell us that there are limitations as to what they can be after the end of the school day? Why not connect with the local youth organisations? Present the challenge to the young people: How could they develop these spaces to make them a place that people want to go to? The skills of creating a programme, marketing, budgeting, and analysing data of previous attendance can feed into a holistic delivery of curriculum areas. With services continually being lost due to a lack of funding, we need to think *broader* as to how we integrate services together so that young people are supported. Projects also provide us with a platform to raise the profile of voluntary services, widening the audience that will see the crucial work that they undertake. Inviting policymakers and stakeholders along to see the final collaborative projects can help us strengthen the recognition of why we need these services in our area.

Social media can be a great way to broaden the student experience. As students and I have worked through projects, we have found we have gained great insight from individuals across the globe. Through the social media platforms that I have created, I have been able to build a network of professionals within the field who frequently offer support to one another. If students have a question to pose, they can use these platforms to ask a wider audience, and you often find that those professionals who are active on social media in a professional capacity are often passionate about what they do and want to offer help to those just starting out. Adopting a holistic and collaborative approach to finding connections to support you in your projects can be done from inside the classroom; it is about thinking creatively as to how you get there.

## Resources

When my daughter was first sent her university's list of equipment she required, it all looked pretty straightforward. The county we live in is largely built on three main economic areas: agriculture, hospitality, and engineering. Surely it would be a doddle to get her engineering equipment. Oh, how wrong I could be! Finding steel-toe cap boots for a female size six foot proved impossible, and we were reluctant to order such a heavy boot online, unable to try it on. At the time, exhausted from this process, I put out a tweet about how frustrating this was, and it was later included in Caroline Criado Perez's newsletter. Caroline Criado Perez (2019) highlights how women live in a world that is designed for men and the importance of recognising the invisible barriers that prevent equality. Reviewing how accessible our resources are for projects is an important task for us to undertake from the outset.

Before we introduce any new projects, we must consider whether we have the resources and understanding for their implementation. The experience must be accessible for all students, and the practicalities will need to be continually reviewed by you, as the facilitator. There are different ways we could approach this barrier for the slim-footed engineer. We could contact some stores and explain that we have X number of students each year and stocking shoes would be beneficial for both parties. We could source them ourselves, absorb costs (you'll be lucky if your budget allows for this!), sell them at cost price to students, or this could be a mini project-based learning (PBL) project for one group of students. When we find ourselves presented with a problem as educators, it can prove highly beneficial to bring this back to the student group. This particular problem would make for a great introduction to PBL in your induction month, reviewing the resources needed for future work experiences and any factors that need to be accounted for. Students are also much more likely to be open about barriers in this framing than when told by their mother in the fifteenth shop that they should send off an email to the course director and all local shop owners on the barriers females face when entering into the world of engineering (here ends the feminist mother's rant; I appreciate the opportunity to write these words down!). But in all seriousness, when we are faced with real-life practical problems, there are no better people to turn to than the individuals who have experienced them firsthand. If we are supporting students towards economic prosperity, they need to be able to problem-solve, be open listeners, and understand when someone else in the team is being restricted from being able to carry out their duties.

## When projects get forgotten

There can be a lot of excitement when a new project commences, but how do you keep the momentum going? When a project is in its infancy, time is often allocated to explore direction and purpose, but it can be very easy to get caught up with other activities and forget the reasoning behind why you chose to adopt the PBL approach. This is why planning is so important to structure the process of how your project will look and the learning intentions that will be covered. Just like a standard lesson plan, a project requires a clear and coherent start-middle-end. Your ending may involve progression onto further investigation and curiosity, but you will still require a pause and for the student to undertake an evaluation and review of the journey completed to that stage. This will allow them to identify how they have found solutions to the initial problem that was presented to them. This is why it is crucial for PBL to be embedded into the curriculum instead of being an add-on, and why teachers need to feel confident in leading projects whilst feeling supported to do so by the wider culture of the education team. The purpose of the projects needs to be understood by the school-wide team so that their relevance is understood and so that you have the time to lead them effectively. Students will soon question why you embedded it in the first place if it is later dropped. Authenticity and relevance are something we will look at in more detail, but these are key factors in ensuring that projects do not become additional or unnecessary work.

**Lack of confidence and independence**

It can be incredibly difficult to lead your own learning when this is not something that you have experienced before. Working in a group requires us to put our ideas forward, and it can be very easy to blend into the background if clear roles and support have not been provided. The lack of confidence and independence is relevant to both students and educators; many of us feel restrained by system processes and have not had the autonomy to express ourselves freely in past experiences. It is important to build trusting environments where people do not feel judged when they share their thoughts. Starting with more anonymised methods of sharing can be a positive introduction; you may wish to begin the year with a short project with students to develop these skills. By refraining from asking students to share their responses to the problem you pose and ideas to overcome it, you could use online tools for individuals to type in their answers, which are then shared as a whiteboard for the group to discuss. Using technology can help break down the barriers individuals may feel when speaking up in a larger group, especially when they may not know many people within it.

Building trusting environments is also vitally important for PBL to work. I have few rules when teaching, instead explaining my values and why I expect our learning environment to be respected in a certain way. The rules I do have are introduced at the start, and I expect them throughout the duration of students' time with us. My first rule is not to speak over someone else when they are speaking. Being an active listener is a skill that is not always fully respected. Pausing and listening to others also develops our own thinking, as others' voices are a catalyst for where our own future direction goes next. Whether we agree or disagree, we need to listen to others, and no one's voice is more valuable than another's; talking over someone else implies that it is. One of my other rules is that we encourage one another. There are times when all of us reply with the wrong answer. If this is met with judgement or sneering, it hurts deeply and instantly creates a barrier to engaging further. Life has enough challenges; when we are together as teams, we must be each other's champions and support one another. None of us have all the answers, and generally, we will all find different areas more difficult than others. By working as a group and helping one another, we not only feel more confident in the next task but also build on our independent skills, as we know that we have a group of people surrounding us that want us to achieve. Approaching projects in this way encourages independence and creates an environment where people feel confident enough to challenge in a productive and kind way, whilst also valuing that new ideas can generate further ideas, engaging us in the learning process and wanting to seek out information.

Angela Chung, an educator from Hong Kong, spoke to me about the importance of students being provided with adequate time to come up with solutions. As students there are not familiar with educational systems where they take the lead in generating ideas, it is important for teachers to invest time to encourage creative thinking, which in turn speeds up the process as students' progress and builds confidence in future projects. Making sure that you clearly outline why you are embarking on the project and how it will support students in their educational journey will develop students' awareness of how their interactions and leadership will lead to positive outcomes. Celebrating their interactions will help build their confidence and help them see the value of independent thinking.

## Resistance from students

It is easy for us to get used to learning in a certain way, and we can find change difficult. It can be very easy to stick with the status quo and guide students through curriculum content, as we then know that everything we need to cover is included in the yearly plan. With considered planning, facilitation, and evaluation, we can ensure that the content is covered, but how do we tackle the resistance of students to having to step up in projects? Building a culture in which questioning is encouraged and feedback is provided at each step by you as the facilitator will help students to change their negative mindset and develop more confidence in their work on the projects. We need to focus on intrinsic motivations for students and start with small goals set by them. Resistance often stems from fear of the unknown, and when learners are asked to take on more responsibility, that can trigger many different emotional responses. Talking about these responses as a collective can help us manage them more effectively and help students see that all of us as humans feel nervous and have to find strategies to manage how we deal with them. Mental health and education go hand-in-hand; if we have low self-esteem, it will influence our ability to respond to something new with a positive mindset. Being more open in discussions and explaining clearly the rationale of the projects will lessen levels of resistance. For students who have been disengaged from traditional modes of learning, PBL can be a really useful tool for changing perspectives and showing how engagement can positively impact their opportunities in later life.

### Fear of getting it wrong

This is relevant for both students and educators. No one wants to be the person to put themselves out there and get the answer wrong, but, as we have considered throughout this book, there is not always only one way to interpret information, and if we do make a mistake, this can offer a great learning opportunity. As educators, we can find ourselves worrying about negative feedback, which is a justified response if received. As a student, there is a fear of looking like an outsider to the group. Both of these responses are human, and we must take into account how we cultivate a growth mindset with both staff and students. First and foremost, I write this book as an educator, and I am not embarrassed to admit that I often get things wrong. It is how we respond to this that matters, and as an educator, it is part of my job to role model behaviours for those I work with. A mistake is a learning opportunity, and we need learners to see how it can lead to greater understanding. We also need to recognise that a mistake is not the end of the world. I have no problem with my mistake leading to a chuckle if the response is underpinned by our collective values of kindness.

### Making sure that curriculum content is covered

We touched on this when considering the resistance that we might meet from students in relation to PBL. But it is important for us to reflect on this barrier in further detail. PBL is a professional and innovative approach to teaching that needs careful consideration to ensure that we still meet the curriculum framework that we work towards with students. It is our responsibility to ensure students are provided with the opportunities to do well in their end-of-year exams and assessments. For younger children, we need to prepare them for their next stage of education. It would be lovely to be able to be completely led by children's own curiosities, but PBL is not an airy-fairy add-on. It is a serious approach that requires commitment from both educators and students. Students should know clearly what learning intentions are expected to be covered through the project so that they are able to focus their direction whilst being guided by you as the facilitator.

### Organisational resistance

Fully embracing the PBL approach requires flexibility and creativity. With quality assurance processes to meet, it can be scary for organisations to veer away from the methods that are typically used by the staff team. When designing your projects, it is important to meet with the full team to review how this will work for all stakeholders. Knowing your purpose and intentions will help to minimise the worries that may be flagged up and build confidence in others as to why this approach will be beneficial for learners. Sharing your initial plans and designs with awarding bodies from the outset can also be a great way to showcase innovation with those who will be inspecting your provision and also ensure that their requirements are met, alongside the necessary requirements for your setting procedures. When I set out on the PBL journey, I really enjoyed developing a stronger professional connection with the awarding body, as it meant that when they visited the first cohort who had experienced a full PBL programme, they had a great awareness of why we approached areas in a certain way and also why we had adapted parts of the project midway due to our reflections and evaluations of what was/was not working effectively for the student groups. Open dialogue between all involved will break down the resistance from wider stakeholders.

## Behavioural concerns

High expectations for students should be a priority for all educators. With PBL, there can sometimes be the concern that, if students are able to freely choose the way in which they participate in a task, it may lead to mayhem. This is not what PBL is, and it is important for projects to be structured so that students take responsibility. PBL is not an approach to learning that leaves learners with uncertainty; it instead cultivates focus and a desire for progression. Many educators I have spoken to have stressed how the project-based approach has minimised disruptions and engaged students who previously were not engaged in lessons. Autonomy over learning experiences can have a significant impact on how students feel and develop an environment where learning is seen by the group as a positive activity to engage in.

## Presumptions and bias

In 1993, the science historian Margaret W. Rossiter first termed the phrase 'The Matilda Effect' (Harbster, 2020), the bias of people not recognising the successes of female scientists and instead contributing the female's achievements to male colleagues. The effect was named in reverence to Matilda Joslyn Gage, a lecturer and activist who was much ahead of her time. An advocate for women's rights and oppressed groups, she made sure to credit women for their inventions, where male counterparts had previously received credit. Matilda raised those around her and did not shy away from controversy. We live in a society where STEM subjects are still frequently seen as male industries, and we could learn a lesson when reviewing Matilda J. Gage's ethics and practice considering how PBL can support us in thinking as a team and implementing principles where we value the skills and contributions of each member.

Our eldest daughter has followed the pathway of engineering and has already observed the bias that can come between male and female trainees. In fact, on the first day of her journey in engineering, she asked for directions to a lesson, and her question brought some surprise. Instead of being directed to the room for engineers, she was signposted to a subject space that would primarily be made up of female students. I am grateful her confidence remained and she asked someone else for directions. She is not alone; in conversations with her female peers, they have told me that males are often put forward for practical projects over them and that they have to work harder to have their voices heard when in group activities. I do not put any less value on the female-dominated lesson she was directed to, but it was disappointing to hear the presumption that she was heading in the wrong direction.

I have observed female engineering trainees prefer not to participate in projects as they put in the work, then a male peer comes in at the end and gains positive feedback on their contribution, even though it was the females who had pulled the project together. This is why it is so important for us, as educators, to recognise our biases and ensure that we are reviewing projects as they progress. I am talking about personal observations here rather than research, but I have seen firsthand the barriers to engaging in projects that can be perceived as learning when the team does not appreciate one another and people maintain an individualistic approach. Our job, when facilitating projects, is to make sure we do not value more highly the voice that shouts the loudest or the one that makes decisions that align with our own responses. We must, instead, factor in ways to explore different perspectives and provide marks and positive feedback for student evaluations that recognise the contribution of peers and show an understanding of how those contributions led to the team's results. What are your biases? It is important for us to recognise and challenge these so that all learners are given the chance to excel.

## Approaching blue-sky thinking differently

I am sure that all of us working in education will appreciate how frequently we hear questions such as 'Why is the sky blue?'. There was a stage in my son's life where he could manage at least 20 questions such as this in ten minutes and expect my brain to work as fast as Google with a full explanation of the answer to his question before he immediately moved onto the next one. Sometimes my answers were not satisfactory, and I was in trouble if I had not listened properly and was caught out as being distracted. We learned together as he grew to home in on the questions that left him most curious and explored the answers together. I am not Google; in fact, take me to a table quiz and you will regret your decision to have me on your team! But what I can do is seek information; I think I am quite good at that, and his curious questions have brought me much happiness as we slide down a rabbit hole together. There are times when not having the answer to something can leave us frustrated. The many barriers that come with learning can be incredibly challenging, and sometimes we can feel as though we are lost in the darkness. When astronauts look down at the world, the atmosphere they share with us is like this: We see the world surrounded by darkness, but what they see is actually something called a sky glow, a light, permanent aurora, further lightened by the reflections of star dust and faint stars. Where there is darkness, there is always a path; sometimes it is just much more challenging to find. Our job as educators is to sprinkle that star dust along the path of learning opportunities. And if you are wondering where I got that snippet of information from, it was from curiosity – a question on the colour of the sky – where distractions were ignored and knowledge sought together. We need to be observant and see where curiosity is shown and how individuals' interests can be a spark for learning.

# 7 Widening students' community and experiences

When I was pregnant with my second child, I was posed with the question in my academic studies, 'are siblings or parents more influential to learning?' As I researched and cradled my baby bump, I wondered how this new little one would be led by her big sister. The impact of peer learning is something we do not always focus on as educators, but it is important for us to evaluate, especially when designing projects. As educators, it can feel uncomfortable to take a step back, but this is the essence of project-based learning (PBL) and widens the connections that students can find to enhance the projects they are working on.

Students should be offered opportunities to engage with a wealth of external influences, and although pre-decided curriculum outcomes are in place, the meaning of these is not transferred in a prescribed manner. Students reflect on their discussions and thinking with others to develop new lines of flight (Deleuze and Guattari, 2004) within their projects and create individual approaches and fluidity to their educational experience. In 2022, the students I worked with at the time were finalists in the Association of Colleges Beacon Awards for Social Action, and this had been gained by shifting the narrative as to how we approached our studies over the students' two-year course. Instead of developing a typical portfolio of evidence, students used reflection, creation, and presentation skills to develop an intergenerational space for children in the local primary school and older generations to come together for learning and social interactions. To show how the project connected students in new ways with the wider community, some examples of how this was adapted are shared in the following. To note, when using the PBL approach, all of the activities are integrated into one project and adopt holistic integration, where the student continues to build on their past knowledge to extend this with the new learning generated. In this project, the students were working towards a qualification to be qualified as an early years' educator, which determined the overall topics identified to be covered through the project. The link between each activity was agreed upon by students, and consideration was given as to what they wanted to work on through each stage:

DOI: 10.4324/9781003424345-8

| Topic: | A typical approach usually adopted for collecting evidence: | PBL approach adopted: | Partners collaborated through the PBL approach: | Examples of evidence collected: |
| --- | --- | --- | --- | --- |
| Health and safety | Review legal and placement requirements for H&S and explain these in a written report. | A meeting took place with the team responsible for H&S in the organisation. Legal and organisational requirements are recorded by students. Leaders from the primary school and the senior group met to discuss further requirements, with information shared on how this is approached in their own work. | Health and safety officers Child protection officers Caretakers Head teachers Primary school teachers Managers and leaders of voluntary and statutory agencies | Risk assessments. Permission letters for parents and carers were created. Video made for parents and carers that included how H&S would be maintained during each session. Reflective journal that included research on requirements. Reflective log on learning through this process. |
| Early years curriculum | Identify the curriculum that is followed for early years and outline the different areas. Evaluate how this is implemented by the early years educator. | Students research the curriculum and decide how they can build intergenerational play activities where a different curriculum focus is in place each session. | Primary school teachers Leaders from the senior groups Children and older people | Plan, do, review. Each session was implemented with different stations led by the students. Photographic and video logs (child protection requirements underpinning this) were used to record the learning that happened from this process. Activity bags were created that students could use in future employment and in their placement. |

*(Continued)*

| Topic: | A typical approach usually adopted for collecting evidence: | PBL approach adopted: | Partners collaborated through the PBL approach: | Examples of evidence collected: |
|---|---|---|---|---|
| Early literacy | Research evidence on early literacy and develop different activities to promote this area of development whilst in placement. | At the start of the project, it was identified that speech and language should be a focus, as outlined by the primary school. Students met with professionals to learn more before creating their own resources to use during the intergenerational sessions. They also decided to create digital resources that could be used by children and the older generation outside of their time together. | Speech and language therapists<br>Midwives and health visitors<br>Librarians<br>Primary school teachers | Story sacks were created.<br>Storytelling: recorded and evaluated<br>Reflective logs that included research (both digital and written, subject to student choice).<br>Online resources. |
| Partnership working | Review the different professionals you will work with as an early years educator and reflect on how each partnership can be developed effectively. | Presentation of learning throughout the project: students hosted a seminar to share their knowledge and learning with professionals. Thirty professionals attended and were highly impressed with the seminar, adopting some of the approaches shared by the students in their own settings. | All professionals who have a childhood focus<br>Council representatives<br>Headteachers and teachers<br>Early years professionals<br>Students studying towards similar qualifications | Presentations and recordings of students leading the seminar<br>Feedback gathered from attendees.<br>Social media posts and blogs.<br>This topic is one where you can see how it also naturally integrates into other areas and is recorded throughout the project. |

| | | | |
|---|---|---|---|
| Well-being | Evaluate how the placement that is being worked on promotes children's well-being and review evidence-based literature on the importance of supporting this area. | As with the curriculum activities, well-being was also integrated, and students partnered up with other vocational areas such as hair and beauty, hospitality, and the sports departments to design physical and emotional well-being activities that would benefit both children and older people. | Students and teachers from other curriculum areas<br>Primary school teachers<br>Parents<br>Professionals relevant to the area | Blogs and videos focused on the research<br>Mental Health Week social media posts<br>Leading well-being activities during the session and evaluating the process. Feedback from attendees is reviewed within this. |
| Reflective practice | Create a PowerPoint on different models of reflection and then record reflective entries using one of the cycles. | Students undertake their research and identify what works effectively for their activities. A journal (digital or written) is maintained by the student throughout the project. | All of the professionals who have been involved in your activities to date – the feedback from professionals – is a useful tool for deepening the reflective process. | Reflective journal (digital and/or written). This tended to be more creative than previous records, with the use of art and creativity used more frequently to express the process of reflection. |

This particular project adopted a long-term approach that would evolve throughout the year. As progress happened, the project evolved to accommodate student autonomy, but there still had to be a clear beginning, middle, and end. We knew that areas such as health and safety would require very clear direction, but the shift in how it was approached meant that students were still able to take the lead and that they also fully understood the process and the purpose of why we had to follow procedures in a certain way. The experience of this group was different for the next year and the year after that, but the overall project maintained the same focus and a clear direction. The main aim of the project was to lead an intergenerational café once per month, but you can see from the aforementioned table just how much can be covered through a technique such as this. There are a lot of additional elements of the project that I have not listed that were also completed, but I hope that by sharing this, it gives you some insight into how a project may look for the students you work with.

Western society sees generations segregated in their learning before a child even begins their compulsory education years. The tendency to stay within our generational peer groups creeps out of this into our social circles, segregating ages from one another and leaving the marginalised feeling unable to have their voice heard across intersections. Adopting community projects, such as the one detailed earlier, provides students with the autonomy to lead their learning experiences and participate in a non-hierarchical process that actively encourages creativity and curiosity. There was a great joy that came from working across generations, and when students shared their experiences with the judges from the Association of Colleges' Beacon Awards, I was blown away by how positively impacted they said they were, not just for learning but for their mental health as well. We need to feel we belong if we are to achieve, and connecting with others is such a crucial requirement for feeling connected in the space where we spend our time.

## Connections across continents

It is always a pleasure for me to talk with educator Angela Chung. Angela lives and works in Hong Kong, and over the past five years, we have partnered on some collaborative projects, teaching early years vocational and Higher Education students together online across the two countries. Angela is currently working towards her masters in human rights and will use this to work towards a fairer education for ethnic minorities living in Hong Kong. Her values are always evident in everything Angela does, and her experiences growing up in Northern Ireland underpin her commitment to ensuring that educational systems promote diversity, equity, and inclusion. Angela spent her childhood in Northern Ireland and felt some stigma at school due to not seeing other ethnicities in her class community. Being ethnically Chinese, she found it difficult to fit in, but she was well supported by her teachers and made good friends during her school years. Moving to Hong Kong, she did not want her children to feel different from others due to their race and heritage, and this impacts her vision for her ambitions in her future professional role. Work has brought Angela and me a strong friendship, but she is also an incredible teacher who wants to make a difference. I was grateful for the opportunity to debate our experiences with PBL and compare and contrast how it has been used across Hong Kong and the United Kingdom.

Although Hong Kong is quite a small city in size, it is home to approximately 7.4 million people. Angela describes Hong Kong as a vibrant and diverse city and explains that there are a great variety of school systems used. Similar approaches to the United Kingdom can be seen, such as Steiner and Montessori being popular models for families choosing early years educational settings. It is important to note that settings are very localised and change across districts. What Angela experiences may be different for those living in other areas of the country. Angela reflects on the first pre-school setting in her area that embraced PBL and how they used this to connect young children with their community by going out on excursions to investigate and learn about the world around them. Settings that adopt PBL take into account their environment, and Angela talks about the free flow seen within these settings and how the beauty of the environment is used to encourage exploratory learning. The trips that Angela mentioned were based around the children's own interests and ideas, giving the children the autonomy to lead what happens during the school day and widening the environment further in which they explore. We have also engaged in PBL activities as we have shared ideas across the globe. Team teaching took place when we were both delivering a child development module with early years students. Students put together resources to share with one another on our country's own educational system, and we presented our research via an online class. What I have noticed through this collaborative approach, which is an important element of this shared learning experience, is that it begins with students viewing the approaches as very different before they recognise our common goals and similarities. It also prevents us from being too insular in our outlook by taking inspiration from peers from around the world.

## How do we find connections?

There is a lot to be said for being approachable and kind! One of the things that students have seen through the projects I have worked alongside them on is how frequently I have had the opportunity to connect with professionals that I may not have seen for a number of years. We focus as a group throughout the year on our professional identity, and it is important to note that this is not someone different from who you are in your personal life but instead someone who carries the same values but considers which elements of ourselves we feel safe and secure sharing when working. Consistently living your values and adopting them in your work will make you someone that others will feel comfortable reaching out to, and you will also feel good about connecting with them on your projects. We have looked at how to make connections in previous chapters, but it is worth noting that, as students see this role modelled, they will feel more comfortable doing this independently and will recognise the importance of modelling kindness and positive communication when working in partnership with other professionals.

### Realisation of what education is like 'in the wild'

Peter Shukie works in Higher Education in England and describes how PBL breathes life into theory. During my research, he shared with me that PBL is consistently and powerfully implemented into the degree programmes he works on and how this provides an experiential exposure in learning where students can experience how to be a designer, collaborator, and leader. The focus on community is evident throughout Peter Shukie's responses on the value and impact of PBL, and in 2019, the work was recognised with a WEA Social Impact Award. Projects have included period poverty, ESOL in taxis, and sustainability in primary schools. This diverse and responsive range of projects brings new life into education and, as Peter shares, brings 'a realisation of what education is like in the wild'.

Peter is aware that barriers such as institutional practice, where more traditional forms of student engagement, attendance, and submission of evidence need to be overcome in the lecture-style environment. Drawing on community, Peter identifies how we need to recognise diverse values and the importance of educators creating spaces for students to encounter and find value in each experience. Peter Shukie notes how adopting an empowering approach can lead to future opportunities and reflects on how one student project has now become an art therapy business and has gone on to win a Queen's Award in 2022.

### The voice of the student

Following are some quotes from students who participated in the intergenerational project that is described within this chapter, and it felt like a good place to end this chapter and summarise what they gained from participating:

> I am at the end of my first year and I thought the intergenerational cafe was amazing. I liked that I could see how children were developing and that my work was contributing to that. I wouldn't have thought about standing up to present in front of others before this year and I've spoken at a conference and played the piano at the cafe which everyone seemed to really like.
>
> As the weeks progressed, I could see children getting quite competitive in their work, they liked the play activities we had designed. I saw the children developing a lot of respect and dignity for the older people and I valued that.

After the seminar two Head Teachers came up to me and said they had never presented at a seminar before. I can't believe I've had this opportunity already.

My Granda has come along to the cafe this year and it has been really nice for him to see what I do and be part of a project I'm working on. I didn't expect my relatives to be at things at college so this has been nice for him getting to know my friends and teachers.

Planning learning in this way has given me so much. We were able to try things out and explore our ideas. This will definitely help me in the future.

# 8 Project-based learning in early years

Across Western society, we frequently adopt a tracking system approach to monitor children's educational progress through stages. Adopting this method takes on the ideology of a universal child, not considering the different experiences or social contexts of individual children. The understanding of children's development has been shaped by developmental psychology perspectives, but O'Dell (2010) argues that these create a bias with particular cultural circumstances underpinning the expectations. A social constructionist stance on this argues that this adoption within practice can lead to the cultural context of childhood being forgotten. Woodhead (1999) argued that this perspective on children's development endorses certain cultures, leading to the promotion of the Western child. The method of testing and rating children's mental abilities through psychometrics was argued to be a decisive factor in segregating children into those with the expected ability and those without. If practice is approached with a universal model, many children can end up forgotten and not given the support they need. Practitioners and policymakers must be reflective in their practice and challenge assumptions that are made about children. A move from traditional discourses where children are viewed as passively moving through development must be challenged for the child's voice to be heard through both research and practice. As children begin their educational journey in the early years, we want to create a space where all children can thrive and where they feel the sense of belonging that is so crucial for our development and progress.

## Collaborative working

Abigail Carr began her career as a nursery nurse in the United Kingdom, completing her degree in early childhood studies before relocating to Hong Kong. She has now lived in Hong Kong for 18 years and progressed to complete her teacher training and kindergarten principal certifications after relocating. Since then, she has worked in kindergarten education. During the COVID-19 pandemic, Abigail set up her own business and now works as a parenting coach and teaching consultant. Her wealth of experience has brought her many skills and expertise to share with others, and it was good to listen to Abigail share the two-pronged approach of working with both schools and parents.

DOI: 10.4324/9781003424345-9

A focus of Abigail's training for schools is on communication and how teachers can utilise play and learning opportunities to enhance their literacy skills. This adopts a holistic approach, with Abigail encouraging educators to evaluate how social interactions during activities can be used to support further development. Many of the schools that she works with adopt the early years foundation stage framework that is used in the United Kingdom, so moving into a new academic year, Abigail is designing training to support teachers in the implementation of this curriculum. In her previous teaching and managerial roles, Abigail has observed how you can meet curricular expectations by integrating projects through playful activities, balancing outcomes with quality play provision. The children still use pencils to write, engage with books, and learn early numeracy, but they do it in a way that suits their needs and comes from what motivates them. Bridging the gap between academic studies and play has been an approach that Abigail has found beneficial for meeting everyone's expectations.

In Abigail's work, she puts an emphasis on the importance of working in partnership with families and on the need for educators to reflect on the expectations that parents have of their children's school experience. She mentions how positive it has been for her own development to work with parents, and she can bring this back to the training and coaching she delivers to educators. Abigail recognises that the experiences parents have with their children will contrast with those that are had in the classroom. She is aware that it can require educators to do additional work, such as providing parents with literature and resources to show how your approach is adopted, but she emphasises how important this is for working in partnership and valuing the expectations of parents so that they engage from the outset and feel their voice is being heard.

We discuss Abigail's work when she was a manager and teacher within a kindergarten. There were two sides to the kindergarten, with Abigail responsible for the English department and another manager having responsibility for the Chinese department. Project-based learning (PBL) was being used within the Chinese department, and Abigail was brought in to support the team in the implementation of this due to elements of the projects being run in English. When a kindergarten nursery for two-year-olds was opened, stories were used as the basis for PBL, and children were immersed into the pages through exploratory play that was facilitated around different books. The themes of the books were reviewed by the teachers to evaluate how the learning experiences could meet the expected curricular outcomes whilst promoting play and investigation. Following children's motivations and interests, the playground became the story, and when inside, the story continued with the teaching team considering what resources and activities could promote children's creativity and further curiosity around the topic featured within the book. Abigail found that by shifting from how we traditionally use storytime and tabletop activities, immersion into the book showed the true value of play. She notes that the level of engaged play was much stronger than it had been in many of her other experiences in Hong Kong kindergartens. Children created their own stories and used role play, and this was also a great way to engage parents, with them attending the kindergarten to see the end result of the learning the project had stimulated. This engagement acted as a catalyst for further engagement from parents, as they saw the purpose of the project and would continue learning about the book at home with their child. The teaching team shifted from using traditional forms of teaching to facilitating the process of learning, with much consideration given to the resources and experiences that could be used as a way of encouraging children to investigate with their peers. Paperwork was shared between the educators and parents to explain the steps that had been taken to scaffold children's development, and this is a useful method for educating parents on how they can do this when the child is in their home environment. Moving away from a focus on daily table-top activities was also useful, as parents saw the process with resources left out for longer periods of time and not packed away prior to their arrival. This meant they could spend time during pick-up exploring the different areas of the setting with their child. When reflecting on what Abigail saw as one of the stand-out moments from implementing PBL, it was the way in which staff from the English and Chinese departments became more integrated and adopted a collaborative approach across the two sites.

Abigail reflects on when she was working with parents during the lockdown periods, when parents were having to educate their children at home. When Abigail works in her coaching role with parents, an important aspect is the role of active learning and how parents can engage their children in learning experiences to promote their child's development. She was pleased when local Hong Kong kindergartens were encouraged not to shift to online teaching during this period of lockdown and showed parents how they could use their daily lives to integrate the learning outcomes that their children would be working towards, if in attendance. It reminds me of my role as a development officer for the childminding sector and how valuable the home learning experience is. Being home-based allows for exploration of our local communities and investigation into the world that the child feels safe and secure within. Building the relationship between educational settings and homes strengthens the experiences that children can engage in and enjoy. Koru is a Māori word for an unfurling silver fern leaf, representing growth, strength, peace, and new life. The visual metaphor can act as a reminder to us of the unfolding of knowledge and is often used in education to represent the creative process of the learning journey. Spiralling learning, as the leaf does as it develops, is a way we can take note of and draw inspiration from what is around us and find possibilities through the simplicity of resources and imagination.

## Caroline Pratt and the city and country school

I read Caroline Pratt's (2014) book 'We learn from Children' several years ago, and it shaped my journey moving forward, showing me how PBL was not a new approach and is one that can be integrated and applied in a sustainable way. Caroline Pratt had a vision that schools should fit the child rather than the child fitting the school. After feeling frustrated with her experiences with schooling systems, she set up her own school that aimed to develop creative and independent thinkers. The school was set up in 1914 and is still going strong today. It brings me much pleasure to follow the social media pages of the school and see how they engage children with innovative and exciting ways of learning. One way that Caroline shifted the way children learned was by introducing nature studies. Instead of children learning about different areas of nature within the classroom, they headed out to explore and investigate. Children would watch the waggons coming into the city from the countryside, observing how produce came to the market. Children would sit by the river, observing the tugboats coming in, and the teachers would facilitate further learning based on the children's curiosity from their observations. Caroline believed that open-ended resources would allow children to engage in play where they were able to recreate the world around them and designed the unit-block, a set of wooden blocks similar to Friedrich Froebel's wooden blocks. These were used by the children to represent the world around them and engage in open-ended investigation, often building parts of the city and the bridges that they saw whilst out exploring. Within the school, the children set up their own printing press, creating a newsletter that would be circulated, and the skills developed by putting this together required the full team's contributions to make it a success. In the early 1900s, there would have been a clear divide as to what types of activities girls and boys participated in whilst in attendance at conventional schools, but Caroline's school saw both genders participating in woodwork, learning how to craft their own resources. What always strikes me when I return to Caroline Pratt's work is how her vision is what we still strive for today. The focus on children rather than systems is one that policymakers could benefit from returning to. In the meantime, we need to channel pioneers such as Caroline Pratt and implement systems that engage and encourage children to explore and investigate the world around them.

### Example of project-based learning for this stage of education

**Personal, social, and emotional development focus:** In my first book on intergenerational practice (Cole, 2022), I wrote about how nursery schools and care homes are frequently hidden away in our community with an emphasis on protection, leading to high fences surrounding the building. I do not dispute the need to safeguard children, but I have found that this design often creates a barrier for different age groups to share spaces and enjoy social time together. A lovely way to develop a project with this age group is by getting out to an area such as community allotments and having children explore what plants they can grow throughout the year. Learning from older residents of the community, children can design their own planters and investigate what is needed for their flowers to thrive. They might want to consider those flowers most beneficial for the bumble bee, surrounding your project with story time and free play sessions that add to the children's understanding of how important the bee is to our environment.

**Physical development focus:** Most nursery spaces will have something growing within their outdoor area, but where can we gain the resources to help these plants thrive? This may be a question that is posed to your preschool group, with consideration given to why water is such a valuable resource. Children can be supported to design their own water collection station for the playground. Resources such as gutter pipes, buckets, and containers can be placed both freestanding and directly onto walls and fences (with support as required), with enquiry encouraged as to which designs gather the most water and how this is best distributed to the plants. Moving away from a weather chart to active engagement with a project such as this can help young children learn more about the seasons and weather variables.

**Language development focus:** Role play is a typical play for children of this age group, and your imaginative play area can be used effectively to explore topics that lead to inquiry. Projects can take the form of storytelling and drama, with children designing their own books and performances on a chosen topic. There is a lot of joy to be found in books created by pupils, and it is a great way to engage children with both fiction and non-fiction texts.

**Early Mathematical experiences focus:** Block play is a wonderful resource for children to use their imagination and their play tools for representation. Building bridges, villages, and skyscrapers teaches children how to explore their own environment and also how to create their own maps, thinking about how we design and what spaces we need in communities. This is the type of project that is important not to pack away at the end of the day but to build on and review as more knowledge is gained by the children.

**The arts focus:** I have often been inspired by the work of Nuala O'Toole (Cole, 2022), who developed the Kindness Postbox during the COVID-19 pandemic. Nuala set up post boxes within shops and schools where people could post letters that would be distributed to local care homes. Children loved using their artistic skills to bring some happiness to other people, and post-pandemic, the Kindness Postbox has continued to grow and develop, with more schools and nurseries becoming involved. Posing the question of how your community connects with one another and the importance of looking out for others provides a good project for this age group, and young children can consider how they can set up and share their own letters and pictures with others.

**World around us focus:** There is something very exciting during the early years about finding a bug to befriend out in the garden, and this can prove beneficial for creating a project that sparks children's curiosity. Bug hotels require little space outdoors and can be made using lots of cheap, natural materials. Children can design their bug hotel and continue to build on it over a period. Consideration should be given to hiding holes for the bugs and any adaptation that may be needed as the seasons change.

# 9 Project-based learning in primary schools

In the United Kingdom, we typically see curriculum areas start to split and be delivered independently of each other. Our focus is to prepare pupils for future tests and exam periods, with children beginning to learn the skill of memorising to support them in doing well in final outcomes. I do not discredit the need to prepare children for what is ahead of them, but I do challenge the idea that this can be achieved by using innovative approaches. Using PBL is a great way to ensure that the divide between achievers and non-achievers is challenged and that children enjoy the process of learning whilst seeing the positive outcomes from gaining new knowledge and skills. Testing that knowledge has been understood is still important within project-based learning (PBL), but adopting this approach prevents us from dictating material to the children to learn from and then finishing the week with a pass or fail examination. Shifting some of your tests to activities such as quizzes encourages peer learning and brings out the positive aspects of competition. When working with primary school children, I once observed a child for over a year who was disengaged with reading, with the teachers seeing the gap widening between the child and their peers. The school was encouraging, providing the individual with additional reading sessions and giving access to a range of different books that were seen as beneficial for the curriculum. What was not initially noticed was the child's interest in the newspapers that sat alongside their learning space and the child's curiosity about the news. When this was recognised, they found the child eager to read, and the pupil began to see the benefits of engaging with reading material. As a parent of three, I am sure I am not the only one who has pulled out the 'Biff and Chip' reading series with a note of despair, knowing that my children will begin trying to read the material with a monotone voice and with no interest in working their way through the pages. I once had a conversation with one of their teachers when they praised one of them for being able to read the book, and I pointed out that they had instead started memorising the page so that they could quickly progress through this stage to the better reading material. A clever technique, although not one where learning is absorbed and digested properly. Reflecting back to the child who engaged with the newspapers, this was the hook to see the purpose of reading and led to the child going off to conduct their own research (with facilitation) on areas of interest they found within the tabloids. The child took ownership of their learning journey and, over the course of six months, lessened the gap between them and their peers on literacy outcomes.

Woodhead (1999) argues that areas such as schooling have just adapted children's learning to a new set of cultural and socio-economic priorities. Where societies without schooling are seen as socially deficient by Western assumptions, schooling shouldn't be viewed as a natural process for learning as it is still controlled by its cultural approach and the priorities of its society. A 'one size fits all' Western model needs to be challenged, and Woodhead (1999) draws on the example of a new model being adopted that values the child and parent in unison, which understands children's psychological value but views this alongside the context of different family patterns. This challenge to practice would mean practitioners and researchers fully understanding the social needs of all those with whom they are working. Education is a fundamental right for all children, and I include Woodhead's (1999) argument to reflect on why we need to work alongside parents and families during this period of learning and value the knowledge that even the youngest child brings to the classroom. When using PBL, we are able to reflect the community values and diversity of the groups we are working with and design projects that are relevant to the social context of each individual.

### How does PBL look in primary schools?

I met with a focus group of primary school teachers who are all engaged with PBL. I want to learn more from them as to how it has enhanced their classrooms and what value they have found in the approach. Teachers saw the project-based process as one where children are immersed in learning and that enhances learning opportunities.

One of the teachers discusses their research journals, a collaborative collection of work where children include their points of interest in one space. This is shared at the end of the year with children in the lower years of the school, with the children presenting their findings and teaching the younger children what they have learned. It is a creative journal where photographs of children's role play and trips are incorporated, and the children choose which ones they want to include in the final book. A narrative from the children is included alongside the photographs and artwork, and the teacher mentions how mathematical skills have been incorporated with charts and information on costs for their trips included by the children.

Another teacher shares how they had two teaching assistants with them last year who had relocated to other countries as part of an exchange programme. This proved a good opportunity to link the curriculum with areas of interest that the children had about the differences and similarities between the two countries. The teaching assistants were eager to support the project and helped to facilitate learning as the children explored different celebrations and put together a cultural day for other pupils to enjoy.

We discuss how PBL has been implemented and consider what needs to be put in place to make it effective. The groups are in agreement that the project must have clear links to the curriculum and that the questions posed are genuine and relate to children's interests and motivations. Linking projects to the community helps to spark curiosity, and the pupils feel empowered by feeling as though they are making a difference in society. Getting parents and families on board, participating in elements of the project, and seeing the end product designed through children's projects helps to work in partnership and encourages children to engage throughout. Teachers mention the need to role model to children how to think critically and show them how to manage their time on the projects so that every pupil understands their role and the importance of teamwork. Differentiating how instructions are provided helps the pupil team understand the context and process of the projects and means that teamwork is maintained throughout, with no individual being left behind as the project progresses. The group agrees that consideration should be given to how you will assess children's participation and achievements, as this can be tricky when a collaborative approach has been adopted. They emphasise that planning and evaluating how you will facilitate the process is important so that projects do not go off track and you can monitor what pupils are learning at each step.

## PBL comparisons within school systems

We previously reviewed the case study of Angela Chung in Chapter 7, and she shared with me further discussion on the routine of pupils in primary school and her observations of how PBL is used with this age group. The primary school experience is different between the United Kingdom and Hong Kong, and Angela explains that teachers will be trained to deliver a certain subject (maths, Cantonese, etc.), and lessons will take place in a similar format to UK secondary schools but tailored to suit the developmental level of the younger children. Although play features heavily in pre-school settings in Hong Kong, once children reach their primary years, the system moves to being very academically heavy, and there is a strong sense that test results and academic achievement are important. This proved problematic when Angela observed children progressing from a PBL kindergarten stage setting to primary school, as children found it challenging to learn in this environment, following a very free-flowing experience in their prior learning. We need to consider this when designing our projects with a two-pronged approach. How do we ensure children are ready for the next stage, and how do we consider that required skills are developed effectively during pupils' time with us? It was interesting exploring this further with Angela. Angela mentioned how transitioning from PBL in the nursery stage to primary is easier when a child moves to an international school, as exploratory learning is still valued and children are encouraged to think creatively when learning. The international schools that Angela works alongside use the Baccalaureate PYP curriculum (IBO, 2023), and within this,

PBL is a common approach used with pupils. Moving away from lessons that require memorisation, children are required to be proactive in their learning and research areas that intrigue them. When adopting PBL, it is valuable to have the children's parents on board and for them to be aware of the process of learning. Angela notes the importance of activities where there are no right or wrong answers, just the opportunity to think outside the box.

International schooling is very expensive in Hong Kong and would be on par with private schooling within the United Kingdom. In both of these affluent educational systems, PBL is frequently used instead of rote learning. The question needs to be asked of policymakers as to whether curriculums are designed for students to excel or to settle. PBL should not be something only for the privileged but an approach that is used throughout all educational models. In curriculums that are static, there are often generic outcomes, and these outcomes are easy to predict. When we embrace curriculums that incorporate creativity and problem-solving inquiry lines for young people, we open up children's experiences, and this should be embedded throughout all of our school systems, not just for a select few. Angela explains that often schools will put on extra-curricular activities where PBL is adopted and that these are in high demand due to wanting children to get the chance to use creative thinking and enjoy play activities. Evaluating how we can balance the wider restrictions with appropriate activities that will enhance lessons should be reviewed as a team and may require us to take some appropriate risks in our approach. Something that Angela found beneficial when training teachers was for site visits to take place so that the trainee educators could see theory in action. Visiting settings that used PBL showed the class group how it aids children's development and learning and identified how they could implement it themselves when they progress into their teaching role. Seeing how effective it can be firsthand means that we can understand the purpose and rationale and recognise how it benefits those participating.

## Further examples of project-based learning for this stage of education

**Science, math, and design and technology focus:** In urban and suburban areas within England and Wales, it is reported that garden ponds make up 20% of all shallow-pond habitats (Howard, 2020), providing spaces for wildlife to thrive, which is declining in more rural areas of the United Kingdom. Pupils can explore how to design and create their own mini garden pond within the school, developing architectural skills and taking into account what resources and habitats would be most beneficial to create a biodiverse environment. Research can be undertaken on which invertebrates and other wildlife are common within the area and the reasons for the decline in some of these in different areas across the country. Consideration will also need to be given to what the best materials to build the mini-pond are, whether this is an old bin lid or recyclable product, along with dimensions, how to ensure animals that accidentally fall into the space can get out, and then a final presentation on the benefits the mini-pond will have on the environment.

**Math, English, history, and the arts focus:** For the final year of primary school, students can be given the project of designing a school for the future where pupils use their experiences to reflect on what they have enjoyed during their time at the school and predict and research wider societal needs for future school communities. A mural, outdoor play area, or part of the classroom can be the main focus of the project, with students designing something that will remain within the school once they transition on, and this will need a clear budget for the pupils to work with. There may be scope for your Parent and Teaching Association to fundraise for this, and an end-of-term event, to present the new space to the children's families and the wider school community can be used as a way of showcasing the pupils learning and for them to present their reasoning as to why they feel this will be a benefit for future pupils at the school.

**Geography and physical education focus:** Feeling a sense of belonging is important for us all, and getting to know our local community is a great way to gain a connection to where we live. To promote this area of learning, pupils can design a walking journey around their area, where QR codes are placed along the route that provide readers with information on the landscape and healthy living prompts. It would be beneficial to involve council representatives to consider how this fits into wider policies for the area, and pupils can learn from them how their plans fit into targets for the area. You could extend this further by including historical commentaries from residents to reflect on how the town has changed and developed over the years.

**Computing and foreign languages focus:** Pupils from the senior section of the school can design an app or activity resource to teach younger pupils a foreign language. Using their knowledge, the pupils can reflect on what is required to learn a second language and also use the skills that they have gained from growing up in the technological age. Pupils can think about branding and how the app can support not just language development but also cultural understanding of the country the language is from.

# 10 Project-based learning in secondary schools

This stage of education is an important stepping stone for young people as they move through their subjects, ready to progress onto Further and Higher Education and employment. None of us should rush through life, but as secondary school teachers, an important aspect is preparing students for this transition and supporting them to get the academic grades and life skills needed for that next stage. There is so much happening for young people at this stage in life, and it can be easy for the student to feel out of their depth if they start to fall behind in subjects. There is also a lot of pressure to memorise vast quantities of information. Pause for a moment at the preparation you put into your own exams at this stage. How much of your revision notes do you remember? How much do you apply to your role now? Do you instead find yourself drawn back to memories of a lesson that hooked you in and caught your attention? We still must prepare the students for the examinations, but with PBL, we can bring to life the knowledge they need for this and relate it to their current and future life experiences.

## The 21st-century skills

There are 12 skills (Battelle for Kids, 2023) that are outlined that young people need to succeed in the 21st century. These are split into three areas: learning skills, literacy skills, and life skills. These skills are as follows, and I would like to explore here how PBL can be utilised to support each of these areas.

### Learning skills

*Critical thinking:* Critical thinking should be part of the goal of your project design. Supporting students to make independent decisions and role modelling to them the importance of backing up your reasoning are fundamental elements of PBL. Throughout each step of designing a project, students make balanced decisions that will enhance the end result. Working out solutions and looking at problems with a creative framing will act as a scaffold for students to build on their prior knowledge and evaluate independently how to increase it further. By working with others, the student will have

DOI: 10.4324/9781003424345-11

to listen and understand other people's opinions whilst also gaining a fresh perspective that could challenge their prior thinking.

***Creativity:*** Students are not provided with the answers in PBL. Instead, they need to become investigators, sourcing information and testing results. As we explore throughout this book, creativity is not just the arts (although they are an important element of the curriculum), but also a way of playing with knowledge so that you can fully appreciate and understand it. Creativity breeds innovation, and young people can engage with learning by presenting information in a variety of formats. This is crucial when the final project showcase is shared, as we do not want students to stick with one style of presentation but instead feel ownership of the wonder of what has been created.

***Collaboration:*** Exchanging ideas and perspectives provides us with time to think through processes together. There are very limited jobs where we will work in isolation; those working in independent roles still require connection with others. I am sure all of us can reflect on a time when we have been in a room with two people who are sure they have the correct answer, only for both to be incorrect. By working with others, we can unpick information and make sense of the world. We can see where we have gone wrong along the way if the end result has not worked, appreciate when others help us, and feel good when we can help them. Being a team player is a required skill for learning and recognises our individual skill set. Life does not require us to herd like sheep, but we do need to be able to actively listen and work with others, skills developed as the PBL team begins to work on their challenge.

***Communication:*** At the time of writing this book, there had been much discussion on the importance of children developing oracy skills throughout their time in education. The Oracy All-Party Parliamentary Group (2021) reports that when pupils engage in high-quality oracy activities, this leads to stronger academic achievement and will boost individuals, social mobility and work opportunities. When engaged with PBL, it is essential for all the team members to communicate, and the presentation and discussions on their final showcase further develop communication skills. We live in a fast-paced environment in modern times, but we must remember the beautiful gift that humans have of being storytellers. Being able to share our stories and communicate with others boosts our self-confidence, and this is very important for feeling secure to learn and explore. Reading, writing, and oral language are approached in unison during PBL, enhancing the learning experience for the student.

### Literacy skills

***Information literacy, media literacy, and technology literacy:*** Creating an environment that is flexible in how project details can be recorded enhances the experience for the students, and integrating technology should be integrated into the design of how the project is captured. As educators, it can be difficult for us to keep up to date as technology evolves, but this has been an area where I have found I have learned alongside students, and we have explored together how it can benefit us and the projects we are working on. In life, we are inundated with information, and students should progress on from us with the ability to make full use of media and understand the messages that they are presenting to us. This is also important as students create their own projects with a critical understanding of what underlies the final work that they are presenting.

### Life skills

*Flexibility*: If we always believe we are right and are resistant to change, it can be very difficult to work with others. Learning to share space and appreciate others' knowledge and opinions will help us grow and feel at ease when working as part of a team. Being considerate of the individuals we are working with is essential here, and our projects should be designed with a neurodivergent approach. This is why a trusting and understanding environment is essential, where changes and adaptations are explained and understood. Understanding the needs of the team and how we can support each other helps us be positive team member. Reflecting on this skill quite bluntly, learning early on which hill we are prepared to die on will help us immensely when it comes to teamwork! It comes back to our values and what is important to us, not just the necessity to have our voice heard.

*Leadership*: A good leader in project-based learning (PBL) will understand the necessity of checking in with the rest of the team and keeping everyone motivated to complete the task. They will recognise the role of each individual within the team and fully understand the shared vision that has been agreed upon. It is also important to remember how collaborative leadership is taking place throughout the project, with individuals responsible for different elements.

*Initiative*: It is very challenging for students to step back from PBL. One of the things that I have found useful as an educator is that students will communicate with each other more effectively around deadlines and ensure that they get their bit to the group on time – not always something that is seen as quite as essential when it is just seen as a submission date set by the teacher! What is wonderful is seeing students grow in confidence and share their ideas, taking the lead on unexpected hurdles and coming up with something new.

*Productivity*: PBL should not be extra work but focused work where individuals are engaged and productive with the task in hand. By having autonomy over the learning process, the student will understand the purpose and take pride in what they are doing. This cultivates productivity, and by having a clear timescale for the projects, they will develop an understanding of what can be achieved during this time. As someone who balances employment with projects such as this book, knowing the importance of recognising when I am being productive and when I am in need of a break is incredibly valuable for giving full commitment to each area. If students can develop this skill in early life, there will be a much better awareness of how we engage in high levels of productivity.

***Social Skills:*** Throughout this book, I have discussed the importance of embedding mental health awareness into the curriculum, and one way of doing this is by evaluating how our projects support social and emotional development alongside academic success. PBL sets the tone for an informal learning space, and although high engagement and quality learning take place, we need to celebrate the social connections that we are making throughout the learning process. When collaborating with both internal and external stakeholders, students will need to reflect on how they engage with other people, and there will be an expectation for them to represent the values that underpin your educational setting. Learning how to interact with different people in different situations will help them develop self-confidence and help them transition from your school. We also need to enjoy life! The social side, where the team enjoys the time of company with each other, helps to build trust and shows the significance of learning. If we want students to become lifelong learners, there has to be fun as part of the journey.

Although the PBL approach is not a new concept (as we saw in Chapter 1), we still lean towards a teacher-centred approach in school systems. Learning is no longer just about acquiring knowledge, and we need to develop 21st-century skills so that pupils have the capacity to feel able to succeed once they leave compulsory education and progress into employment.

## Learning the Mandarin language through PBL

As part of my role at the college where I work, I am employed as a teacher and learning advisor. In this role, I work with teachers who have relocated from China to the United Kingdom for a one- to three-year period, and I discuss with some of the teaching team their experiences of PBL when teaching language lessons. This has proven a positive approach, as it has engaged students in understanding the cultural aspects of language learning. Projects such as creating a guidebook for tourists have been created, along with writing a poetry book and putting together performances to share with peers outside of their language lessons. Students who can travel to China are able to immerse themselves in the language and are able to create travel logs, both through blogs and vlogs, to share their experiences with people at home and include information on the language they are learning. Pupils in the younger years of secondary education enjoy putting together dance routines and songs that can be shared with others, where moves represent the pinyin characters. Teachers express that by using PBL, the pupils develop a respect for multilingual and multicultural experiences and enjoy learning more, recognising the similarities across the different countries and regions. I am sure many of us can appreciate the contentment and conversation that comes from sharing mealtimes and some of the teachers share how they have co-taught with colleagues working in the Food Technology Department where children design meals that integrate ingredients from both China and Northern Ireland, creating authentic and new dishes to share at the final event. Whilst the different projects are being worked on, other subject areas are integrated naturally. We can see how the guidebooks could be a collaborative project with the geography department, or poetry and artwork could be shared with the English literacy teachers. The team agrees that adopting PBL enhances the experience and brings fun to the lessons with the older pupils. They want to engage, and the teacher is able to scaffold their learning by explaining grammatical placement and extending vocabulary as they work through their activities. As previously mentioned, the teachers have not been working in the United Kingdom for a very long time, so this is also a beneficial way for them to learn from their teaching peers and for teachers to learn from one another as they share the facilitation of the lessons.

**Examples of project-based activities for this stage of education**

**Literacy and social science focus:** 'Banned books'. What do the books 'Charlotte's Web' by E. B. White, 'Little Red Riding Hood' by the Grimm Brothers, and 'Maus' by Art Spiegelman have in common? The subtitle of this section should provide you with a clue, but all three of these books have been banned for children in some American states. I will leave you to undertake your own research as to why these books were banned, but when approaching reading materials with young people, a sure-fire way to spark curiosity is to let them know that the books you would like to explore with them are on a censored list. Identifying one of the books to read and convening as a group to debate whether books should be banned by schools and districts can bring a wealth of discussion, alongside students evaluating the text and designing their resources for their debate, with the possibility of working with the local library to design a 'banned book' display with their literature to share with a wider audience.

**Science, math, and history focus:** It would be lovely if all of the educators reading this book were working in shiny, eco-friendly buildings. My assumption is that not that many of us will be, but what this does give us is the opportunity to explore how we can make our spaces more effective, and there are no better people to reflect on this than those who will be designing our future spaces. Pupils can spend time with the senior management and governing team to review the cost of energy within the school and build a report that provides the leadership team with plans and costs for moving to renewable energy whilst presenting the reasons why this move would benefit the school, community, and wider society. Students can undertake some site visits to buildings from different eras to review how energy sources have changed over the years and the reasons for this, designing spaces for the future that take sustainability into account.

**Geography and languages focus:** Focusing on the United Nations' Sustainable Goals, the students can explore the topics of poverty and rights. Within this project, research will be undertaken on how rights and priorities look across the globe, and consideration will be given to how life is experienced by children of the same age. A video that evidences this and how poverty can be tackled can be put together by the students. They may also benefit from considering our own biases and why our own country's approach may have its faults. For example, if we live in an environment with access to central heating, our families own cars, and we have continual lighting in the buildings we spend time in, is this something that adds to poverty in other parts of the globe? The group should also consider power imbalances and the importance of valuing things other than finances.

**Physical education, science, and citizenship focus:** Social media has lots of benefits, but there are no doubts that the use of filters and the emphasis on perfection online can lead to negative body image ideals and add pressure to our mental health. Students can design a social media campaign that considers how we promote a positive view of who we are and how we take care of ourselves. Nutrition, body image, and community spaces can be explored, with students using the organisation's social media or website page to promote their campaign. Videos can be used as part of this, along with interviews with sports teams and coaches who work in your area.

**Art and design focus:** Students can put together a proposal for local councils that explains the importance of a community space. It may be for the young people themselves or for different groups to come together. Students can consider where in the community the space would be beneficial (this could be on your school grounds) and design both the area and the murals and artwork that will be included to represent the area. These sculptures and murals may also include creative writing displays, with students' poems and contributions included within the space to add to the creativity.

**ICT and citizenship focus:** Passing on our skills to others is not only an important tool for paying back to our community, but it is also a beneficial way of thinking through our own knowledge and recognising any gaps. An intergenerational approach can be adopted here, with the project focused on students running workshops for senior members of your area where they teach how to use ICT equipment or a particular app. Being partnered with a senior participant, or working with a small group of attendees, is a great way to encourage those who are usually quieter in the group to gain confidence in communication and build on their leadership skills.

# 11 Project-based learning in further and higher education

In the United Kingdom, we are seeing a greater emphasis on project-based learning (PBL) being used within Further Education. This is with good reason, as at this stage of education, students are preparing to enter the world of employment, and it is our duty, in Further Education, to provide them with the skills and expertise to transition into work with vocational competence and confidence in their own abilities. I feel privileged to work with students in this category, and it is a joy to see the learning we do together progress into a variety of roles in the sector in which I have worked and which I hold in high esteem. PBL is an approach that fits naturally with Further Education and should be used on all courses. Moving away from traditional portfolios full of essays and instead meeting with employers to experience the reality of their vocation will not only give the students insight into their future role but also build analytical and evaluative skills that will deepen their understanding of the knowledge taught on the course.

At this stage of education, students are engaging in work experience, and we have the professional relationships with employers to build on this connection and widen the student experience. Meeting with employers and explaining the reasoning behind the approach and how it can help their organisation makes it a beneficial addition to this already established relationship. There should also be consideration as to how departments across your own college can link together, and the examples within this chapter provide practical examples on how to make this work. A holistic approach, where both vocational teaching teams and cross-vocational areas work together, deepens the experience for students and also supports our own professional development as we learn from others.

## A whole college approach

I first met Michaela Greaves through the community of practice, JoyFE. The online community brings people from Further Education together to share ideas and support one another in a non-hierarchical manner. Immediately upon meeting Michaela, I knew how real and inspiring her work in education is. When interviewing Michaela online to discuss her experiences with PBL,

I felt excited by the energy and innovative mindset she shared with me, and it was evident the approach is making a real impact on the college where she works.

Michaela works at Chesterfield College in England and has been working on a 'leading from the middle' professional development programme through the Education Training Foundation. This led to her evaluating the pedagogical approaches used within the team and reflecting on how they can enhance the learning experiences for students whilst also raising the confidence and innovation of educators. Michaela has been instrumental in bringing educators from an array of subject areas together to work more collaboratively and consider how what used to be thought of as 'soft skills' are actually skills required for moving confidently into a vocation. Through a programme embedded by the college called ASPIRE, educators have been undertaking action research and following their own individual journeys to enhance their pedagogical approach before bringing this back collaboratively for others within the college team to learn from. Midway through this academic year, the team held a professional development day with a difference: A 'Be Curious' fair was held with different vocational teams sharing their findings and projects for others to review, and Michaela tells me how much staff's confidence has grown from this new pathway for professional growth. Michaela says how this individual approach has been a key feature of the programme as staff have had to embrace the process of research, with professional development not being done to them but instead something they have actively sought out and which has been led by each member of the team. From this, the ASPIRE programme brought new thinking as to how whole-college approaches could be adopted that focus on the same goal but with the individualised thinking of vocational teams, whilst also meeting the vocational areas' specific learning outcomes. In 2022, at the beginning of a new academic year, staff, students, and governors all pledged a commitment to the college's plans for sustainability, and these goals were then embedded into the curriculum's planning. The goal is for students, as part of their ASPIRE tutorial programme, to understand the impact of sustainability within the future job role in which they are training. Each team has approached this differently with students, and it is exciting to see how students, staff, and employers have embraced not just PBL but also the pledge that they have made.

Childcare students have made a 'hedge-pledge', creating a nature garden that is hedgehog-friendly whilst also learning the value of outdoor play and learning for young children. This project will be invaluable when they move into employment and focus on the design of outdoor learning spaces. Through storytelling, the students are working with local primary schools whilst they develop the garden, and health and social care students are also gaining stronger connections with their local care homes through the projects on which they are working. Students in another vocational area were gifted second-hand mobility scooters that required repair and were set the task of upgrading them and making them fit for purpose once again. Different departmental groups have focused on particular areas of this project, from making the scooter work again to consideration being given to the paintwork and overall design. In projects from the previous year, hairdressing students built their projects around sustainability in hairdressing and how much plastic is generated in the industry, with students undertaking work to evaluate alternatives. This has progressed further with students developing mats for ocean spillages, and this has stimulated curiosity from students' employers/placement providers. Michaela has noticed that local placements want to know more about how to be sustainable and are asking questions of students about how to approach this after observing the projects on which the students are working. The goal of the hairdressing team is to make their local hair salons plastic-free, and they are planning to role model this approach within the college when they refurbish their new salons. Michaela feels that students are learning the skills needed for industry trends moving forward, and employers are valuing these skills being developed in future employees as they are bringing through the ideas needed to progress to the next level. There have also been other projects resulting from listening to the student's voice, and the team became aware that students with additional needs found a barrier when trying to apply for courses at the college due to the layout of the enrolment forms. Students are now working with the college's Business Support Team to create new forms so that this barrier is addressed and future students will feel more empowered when applying to their desired courses. This awareness that systems need to be reviewed and feedback needs to be gained from service users is such a crucial skill that can sometimes be missed, and it is wonderful to listen to Michaela being open and responsive to the importance of recognising when areas require improvement whilst actively listening to what people have to say.

Michaela has seen an improvement not only in students' outcomes but also in the confidence and practice of the teaching teams. Events such as the professional development 'Be Curious' Fair were not only a great exchange of ideas and skills, but Michaela also mentions how it is a way of checking in and monitoring progress and outcomes. As a follow-up to this event, Michaela and the teams will be hosting another whole college event soon that celebrates the end of the students' and staffs' journeys and highlights what has been learned and valued by each individual team. When asked about the impact this approach has had on staff, Michaela replies that it is the growth of teams that has been the greatest success. Michaela expresses that over a period of four years, it is hard to recognise that some teams are the same people. Confidence has grown, and staff feel empowered to try out their ideas whilst evidencing the outcomes and reasoning through their action research.

### Projects to bring generations together

One of the most successful projects I have been involved in was an intergenerational project, with students' planning and facilitating an intergenerational café. The student's main objectives were to plan activities for primary-aged children that would contribute to their development and engage them in their curriculum using a play-based approach. This project fits well with the *Alexandrite Educational Programme* (a comprehensive overview of the programme is provided in the next chapter) as it incorporates the framework, and more detail on the impact of the project can be found in my book *Intergenerational Practice in Schools and Settings* (Cole, 2022). Students from both Further and Higher Education classes led the cafés, bringing generations together, and they used this project as the basis of many learning outcomes, leading to the group winning a number of awards for their social action and leadership of the project. Assessment of their participation included feedback from attendees, video logs, journals, posters, hand-outs, observation from teachers, presentations, and animations designed by the students to use in the café. They spoke at local Council seminars, at round-table meetings with members of staff and external stakeholders, and with the organisations and schools that were involved in the project. They also presented at global conferences. Moving from the traditional lecture and essay approach to this brought so many more opportunities for students, and underpinning the projects in students' feedback was how much their confidence has grown and the positive impact this approach has had on their mental health. Bringing education to life is what we should all aspire to, and this will support students' holistic development and future outcomes.

## Creating projects for the moment

In April 2022, the Northern Ireland Department of Education announced that they were cutting the 'Bookstart Baby Programme' (Meredith, 2023). This scheme, run by the Book Trust, provided over 20,000 children and families with literacy advice and free books, with every baby born receiving one or two picture books. The scheme was one to promote shared reading between babies and their carers, promoting a love of reading from the early years of a child's life, and this cut meant that Northern Ireland was the only part of the United Kingdom where this scheme would no longer take place. As an early years educator, I was aghast to see the news and reviewed how little this scheme cost the government, reflecting on why this was seen as an area where services should be cut. Research tells us that there is a strong association between a child's early language development and their educational and life outcomes (RCSLT NI, 2022), with currently at least two children in every Northern Ireland classroom having a speech, language, or communication need. The RCSLT NI (2022) reports that this percentage increases to 50% of school-aged children when living within an area of deprivation.

News such as this is disheartening. There is little we can do when decisions are made by those at the top, but this should not prevent us from discussing what can be done and also reviewing, with future leaders, what alternative approaches could be taken. As I was working with a class of Further Education trainee early years educators, this news article was one I wanted to take to them to explore further. There was an abundance of learning outcomes within their curriculum that could be covered here: children's rights, child development, planning activities for literacy, policy-making, working with families, supporting additional needs, and the impact of deprivation on outcomes. Once I had a general idea of which areas we could cover, I wanted to bring this to the student group to discuss. There were a wealth of practitioners we would be able to link with to explore the impact of this cut further, and this would also provide us with an understanding of how this cut may impact wider services. It also gave me the opportunity to show why the knowledge we were learning was relevant and highlight to students what they could do to bridge the gap that the government has left. I had my own views on the scheme being cut; it was important for me to recognise these feelings, take a step back, and actively listen to what the students had to say. My own opinion may be challenged, and some of the group may decide when they undertake their research that if something has to be cut, then this one would have the least impact. They may decide that this service is one that can be easily developed by individuals on the ground, and that the budgets of services could factor this in. Whether or not I agreed was irrelevant. What is more important is that we explore and research this in greater detail and use our classroom experiences to develop skills and build knowledge that will support them to be effective practitioners when they move onto employment.

When using this stimulant for classroom activities, it is important to follow a framework and agree on a timescale as to how long we are to spend on it. This type of project could take place all year as ideas and concepts develop, but that would not have suited our overall curriculum plans and requirements for quality assurance. Factoring in periods for exploration is a great way for you to build in projects that are in the moment, and it can be useful to discuss it with your teaching counterparts to see if it links with any of the learning outcomes they are due to teach so that you can adopt a collaborative approach to the project. Following the project cycle, the project was designed with students following the initial introduction on why this news story was relevant to us and how it related to our learning journey. Students began the project with research: 'What impact would this cut have?' Research included talking to professionals in the sector to gather their opinions on this. Talking to different practitioners allowed it to be linked to specific criteria, for example, the impact the midwife felt it would have on families or the impact the playgroup leader felt it would have on children's development. The student group then had to design an alternative programme that was realistic and easily implemented. Alongside the learning outcomes required for their qualification, this type of project also develops other skills required for employment, such as budgeting, report writing, and collaboration, tying in with the literacy and numeracy courses that students study alongside their vocational qualification. We are still working on this project as I write the book, so I have not yet seen their final project, but I use this example as a way to show how important it is to stay up-to-date with the sector we teach within the Further Education environment. Articles such as this present themselves weekly, and not just for early years. A sector news bulletin noticeboard can be a useful way to promote classroom discussions, and providing yourself with time throughout the year to explore these in further detail can enhance the learning experience whilst keeping the material fresh and relevant. I frequently use part of tutorial time for students to bring their own ideas for learning to us, and it is great to now have it as a staple part of discussions where they bring news stories to us that they feel require review and want to find a way to overcome a wider societal problem that has been identified. Why not give yourself 15 minutes this week to flick through the news, find three reports that you feel fit with your teaching plans, and create a mind map that links these to a range of learning outcomes that students could cover to start on a new project-based classroom activity?

## Further examples of project-based learning for this stage of education

**Design, hair and beauty, and event management focus:** Students can explore the fashion industry and reflect on how these have evolved over a period of time. From this research, their project could be to host a sustainable fashion show, where their task is to evaluate how their clothing lines and event will use sustainable materials and resources. From hair products or food through to clothing, the event will enable local retail and other businesses to come along to learn from the students, with poster boards detailing the way in which their research has underpinned the final showcase.

**Travel and tourism and history focus:** Students will explore their community and evaluate how welcoming it is to tourists, identifying the main spaces that could be made more desirable to visitors. Consideration as to why this would benefit the community and the money this could bring to the local economy will be part of the project for students to present to council and tourism organisations. Literature for tourists can be developed, along with celebrating the cultural diversity within the area and the different events that are held each year. Travel routes can be planned alongside walking tours. The tours could be something that is offered to community groups, with students working with the hospitality businesses within the area to offer deals to the visitors.

**Health and social care and social sciences focus:** As technology continues to evolve, evaluating and designing home safety devices for those living within independent living accommodations can support students in learning about the technology with which they are working and considering how this can be developed even further. Students can talk to managers of those who work in the sector and to those who have designed products that help keep people safe. Literature and videos can be designed by the students to highlight to residents the purpose and usefulness of the different pieces of equipment and resources, whilst also pitching new ideas to businesses and organisations working in this area.

**Engineering focus:** Linking with a local engineering business can be a great way to develop links with industry, and for this example, I would like to draw on the experience my own daughter had when studying for her FE engineering qualification. Not only has her experience with PBL on the programme been an area that she often discusses, but it has proven to be one that is asked more about when she has been interviewed. PBL enhances the curriculum vitae, and I also saw it as the catalyst for my daughter's future career. For her project, she worked alongside her peers, and the company set them the task of re-designing a particular part of rail for a plane part. The students needed to evidence how their design would either save time or money for the business. Each team presented their end product to a team from the company and were provided with feedback on their approach. A journal of progress was kept by the student, and I know from talking to the group in an informal capacity that they gained a lot from this experience and were delighted to hear positive feedback from employers on their work on the project. If you use this approach yourself, the problem or area that the company would like the students to review can be anything that works for them, and you can provide guidance on what you need to ensure learning objectives are covered accordingly. It can also lead to employers getting to know the students you work with better – a great pre-interview for future employment!

# 12 Developing your own sustainable project-based learning experiences

### The Alexandrite FE educational programme

In the spring of 2020, due to the COVID-19 pandemic, we saw life change dramatically as the world closed down and we moved to online learning within our educational settings. It was a period filled with emotions and meant that we, as educators, had to rethink the way we worked. As the months progressed, we saw communities develop online, and we still maintained our sense of connection despite being on screens. For myself, being in Northern Ireland, I had not always had the opportunity to meet with others in the sector from across the rest of the United Kingdom, as there had previously been many barriers, such as the cost of travelling or not being able to justify the time spent away for short seminars. The lockdown period changed this, though, and was certainly a highlight for me during the lockdowns. I was able to attend professional development sessions from across the globe and share practice with others, which developed my skills and knowledge as an educator. This was when I found the community of practice, *JoyFE*. The JoyFE Collective was formed by Dr. Lou Mycroft and Stefanie Tinsley. Sharing daily reflections for those working in Further Education, they also introduced the online *Ideas Rooms*. This is something I will discuss more as we continue in this chapter, but in summary, it is a session for people to bring their ideas and explore them alongside others whilst using thinking environment principles (Kline, 2009). Just prior to this period, I had been working on project-based learning (PBL) programmes, and we wanted to develop this further within the FE environment. I used the Ideas Room to formulate our ideas and begin creating a framework to guide our practice. Although this was designed with the concept of being used within Further Education, as you progress through this chapter, you will notice that it has now evolved further to be used across different stages of education.

### The magpie

In Matthew Syed's book 'Rebel Ideas' (2022), he talks about *rebel combinations*, where two conventional ideas are cross-pollinated to create something

DOI: 10.4324/9781003424345-13

different so that it brings new innovation. There is a lot of amazing practice taking place across education, and one of the best ways to bring change is to weave combinations together to design practice that takes the best bits and places them together in one place. There are often very few new ideas that come; instead, ideas are brought together and evolve, being used in a way that has not been done before. I have always seen this as similar to the behaviour of the magpie bird: collecting up the shiny things to bring back to the pedagogical tree, where best practice underpins the practice that takes place. I am aware that the magpie does, however, get a bad rap for being frowned upon for taking people's expensive, glittery jewellery and brightly coloured coins without a backward glance. Researchers from Exeter University (Shephard, Lea and Hempel de Ibarra, 2015) tested this theory to see if the magpie only collected the superficial materials that shone and found that this was not true. When the researchers placed out different materials, such as nuts, items spray painted matte blue, and aluminium, the birds actually showed signs of shyness around the bright items. The clever magpie instead is able to remember where they stored their food and is able to undertake complex tasks. The magpie is a beautiful gatherer of both the practical and the detail, creating a nestful of inspiration and usefulness whilst travelling alongside his fellow flock (the collective noun for magpies is often referred to as a *mischief.* Interesting how many of us that flock together to bring positive change can also be considered as this!). I am grateful for the magpie for being my inspiration as to how we gather ideas for our pedagogical roots and for the foundation of the approach I will share with you in this chapter.

One area where I cannot take inspiration from the magpie is that he does not appreciate where the shiny and practical things come from, but he is an animal who cannot talk, so we need to give the bird some credit (maybe a salute? I also love the magic and superstitions that come with this bird!). As humans, we need to recognise others, and I hope that within this chapter and across this book in its entirety, I have recognised the many contributors who have influenced the way I carry out my practice and the design of this framework. When we bring together ideas, it is important to refer to the individuals or groups that inspired us, connecting us with values of kindness, integrity, and teamwork. As you read through the framework, you will see where ideas have been stimulated through other people's ideas and research, and it is integral to the framework that everyone involved is recognised for their contributions.

## The alexandrite framework

### Values and principles

The framework is built on the following key areas, and as we go through the design, you will see how these are integrated into teaching, learning, and assessment:

*Principles – proactive – pedagogy – projects – perseverance – prosper – personal*

These values and principles are for both students and educators, and they provide us with the basis for how we work towards our projects. What do these mean to you and the students you work with? This starts us off on our PBL journey, and educators should reflect with their student group as to what the Alexandrite framework values and principles mean to each of them. This can be undertaken in a round-table discussion, and throughout projects, there should be consideration of how the work undertaken is underpinned by these values and principles. The expectations of learners are to progress on from the organisation carrying on the values from their education and integrating these into their future, so it is an important aspect to ensure everyone is aware of their meaning and reflect on how they are woven through the progression of the projects in which they participate.

The programme is built on an ethic of care. The values of the organisation should be integrated into the programme from the outset, and time should be allocated for both staff and students to explore these and engage with their meaning and influence on their role within the educational setting. Departments may choose to then develop further values that are integral to their vocational/subject area, reflecting together as a group on the core values that are important to them and also providing time for everyone to draw on the principle of *personal* and consider what the values most important to them are for progression. This embeds ethics of care from the outset and allows staff to feel truly part of the organisation's community. At the start of the year, I find I gain much more from students engaging in dialogue and journaling about what is important to them than any icebreaker game would, and it helps me get to know the student group better. From my own experience as an educator, this draws on the occupational standards and values of the sector in which I train students and provides me with the space to embed these into all aspects of the students' curriculum and give them the underpinning values needed for their vocation. It is valuable to consider what core values underpin the work that your students will progress in, the underpinning values of roles that relate to your subject area, or maybe your wider school values.

*What's in a name?*

This framework was developed during the lockdown period of 2020. Although rethinking education is not something new, I think many of us, as educators, found this period a time where we were provided with space to design programmes so that students could be better supported both academically and pastorally. Managers had to trust staff and teams to draw on their experiences, and many of us had the autonomy to try out ideas that we had played with in the past but had not had the time to integrate effectively. Our technological skills developed quickly, and we learned how to do things that had not felt possible only a month earlier.

This programme does not 'rethink' what we do but instead embraces opportunities to use every individual's knowledge and skills to enhance the good practice that is already there. There are many excellent teams doing exceptional work, but sometimes getting the time to think creatively together is missed. The aim of *#AlexandriteEDPRO* is to create a purposeful framework that is manageable for teams and encourages collaboration and positive thinking. During the lockdown periods, educators drew on their experience and made brave and exciting decisions to embrace new delivery models, continually learning as they progressed. Both within teams and through collaborative spaces that brought educators together, support was provided throughout the transition to blended learning/lessons from home, and we found *critical friends*, reflecting with one another to consider how approaches could be strengthened in a kind and considered way. This period required us to be vulnerable, brave, and open to testing new approaches and strategies. This led to a range of innovative and exciting new ideas being embedded into student programmes across all levels of education.

The framework got its name from the gemstone alexandrite. This rare and valuable gem is not always recognised for how unique it is. Under different lights, the human eye will see it as different colours. It also includes titanium, one of the strongest metals. When I read about the properties, it reminded me of the strength and persistence of students, along with the necessity to be able to shift from different aspects of our lives so that we can enjoy what we participate in. Being present in what we do is important for our emotional well-being and progression, and as the gem moves from green to red in the darker light, it reminds us to take a break from work and enjoy the evenings with friends and family. The properties of the alexandrite gem are said to provide you not just with the feeling of joy but also the ability to find your own joy within yourself, and it is also said to facilitate an awareness of the beauty of every moment. The gemstone is reputed to provide you with the power to choose and make the most of your life. Finally, the gem is said to provide hope through an awareness of the opportunities available to you, no matter the circumstances. The alexandrite gem is the birthstone of June. Although there are courses that do finish throughout the academic/calendar year, the month of June is when most stages of education celebrate the achievements and successes of so many of the students. The metaphor of growth into the next stage of the students' journey as they progress onto a new year, or new vocation, feels strongly significant to the principles of the *Alexandrite Education Programme*. I appreciate that not everyone will feel such a strong connection to the meanings behind the gems as I do, but even if you do, it shows the value of the need to connect with the natural elements and is a reminder that our responsibilities to nature are essential. The properties and meanings are also deeply important for being a successful learner, and this is where the development of the *#AlexandriteEDPRO* stemmed from. With storytelling being such an important part of what makes us human, this is the story behind the name.

Through the programme, students will gain access to a holistic approach to learning. PBL is at the forefront of students' studies, giving ownership to the individual for their education. The wraparound sessions and continuing professional development opportunities for staff will also provide educators and students with non-judgemental sessions to learn from one another and celebrate the voice of each person within the learning space.

The hashtag is included deliberately. It provides a mechanism for educators to connect via social media to share experiences, ask questions, and celebrate students' achievements. Many of us use social media for our professional development, and including a hashtag can help us gain tailored support across organisations. *#AlexandriteEDPRO* encourages us to think about professional development differently, and this is just one of the ways in which that can be done.

## Supporting staff in #AlexandriteEDPRO

During the design of this programme, it was clearly identifiable that many educators felt that more opportunity for fresh thinking and creativity was essential for designing and delivering successful programmes. Sometimes CPD activities that we participate in can feel valuable, but then staff members struggle to find the time to integrate new learning into practice. We can often be very insular when it comes to our thinking, and we do not get the opportunity to collaborate with other educational settings or educators outside our own organisation. Being able to collaborate with our wider peers can bring great benefit to our learning and the experiences that we can provide to the students with whom we work.

Staff need to believe that they are the experts. By placing value on staff's knowledge and expertise, there will be a boost to productivity and increased happiness in the role. The staff are the key to improving practice and have the knowledge needed to do so. By creating spaces to share knowledge and skills, we develop a culture where we work more closely together and feel more at ease sharing new ideas and resources. All staff need to feel that they are trusted as experts, be given autonomy for creativity/creative thinking, and, in doing so, feel brave to try out new ways of working with students.

The *Alexandrite Education Programme* includes regular sessions for educators to learn together through a blend of master classes, where staff will share their expertise with others as part of formal CPD activities and 'ideas rooms' sessions. The ideas rooms will create a monthly space for staff to come together to 'think out' their ideas for learning and improving educational provision, allowing others to support them in developing their ideas into action. Slightly further on in this chapter, I will explain how these are run and facilitated so that you can implement them as part of the programme. Both of these sessions encourage active listening and time for planning, and they provide staff with spaces for their voices to be heard.

By ensuring all staff have a voice and feel comfortable sharing their knowledge and practice, there is more trust amongst teams. This allows for more of an *open-door* culture for informal peer teaching observations. Regular sharing of delivery is encouraged within *#AlexandriteEDPRO*, and PBL encourages collaboration and more team teaching lessons. To enhance the well-being of teams, there should be methods embedded for regular check-ins between staff, using connection methods such as online chat spaces and thinking pairs. Thinking pairs is a reflective activity developed by Nancy Kline (1999), where partnership and trust is key. Within thinking pairs, two people will actively listen to one another to develop independent thinking. Each person takes turns listening to one another, and it is vitally important for the person listening not to interrupt the speaker and to pay attention. It can help to be in a space where disruptions are at a minimum. This is a time to put the phone away in a drawer and to be present with the person in front of you. Once the speaker/thinker has finished speaking about what they want to share, they will make this apparent to the listener, and the roles will reverse. When the individual responds, it is important for the partner not to offer advice but to instead share their freshest thinking on the discussion. By following these simple but vital rules, this removes a power imbalance and offers the pair an opportunity to create a shared exchange. The thinking pair can take place in a short period of time (20 minutes set aside to pay attention is beneficial here), but the focus and attention can bring a huge amount of clarity.

**Ideas rooms**

The Ideas Room was created by JoyFE and is now a twice-weekly event hosted online and attended by many educators from across the United Kingdom (and sometimes even further afield!). Since its creation, it has been used by many professionals as part of professional development activities or with groups of students. The one-hour session follows Kline's (2009) thinking environment principles, and although there are limited rules, the ones in place are important to follow. The hour begins with a round where each person answers the question 'How are you?' and they share the idea that they would like to think through, or identify if they would like to be a listener during the hour. Once ideas are shared, another round takes place so that everyone can decide on what idea they would like to join in with. Drawing back to the collective values, the facilitator should remind the group before the second round that we do not want anyone on their own, and some people may say that they do not mind what idea they go with to balance out the different groups. This round generally brings smaller groups, and the ideas are reflected on for 45 minutes, with each person sharing their freshest thinking on the topic, continuing to adopt the thinking environment principles (Kline, 2009), where you do not interrupt the person speaking and wait for them to handover to the next person so that you know their thinking has come to a natural pause. It is really important that no one is interrupted to prevent the flow of thinking from being agitated, and advice is not welcome. This can be challenging at times but proves to be a beneficial way of stimulating a variety of responses to one idea, creating insight into how the idea can evolve. There is no place for ego in the Ideas Room; job titles or student roles are not relevant, and everyone's voice is appreciated. If someone does not want to speak, they can pass on their turn to the next person, but the round continues without going back to them, as this can sometimes be used as a power play by individuals. Note-taking is discouraged, and attentive listening is essential. The space requires everyone's full attention, and disruptions need to be minimised for the flow of thinking to take place. Depending on how many people are in each group, the rounds go on until the time draws to an end, and everyone is encouraged to be concise and succinct in their responses to give everyone time to reflect. The purpose of handing over to the next person when you have finished speaking makes it clear that you are content with your thinking and ready to listen again. The only person who will interrupt will be the facilitator of the room if someone else is seen as interrupting someone else's turn. Once the main rounds of thinking on the different ideas have taken place, the room closes with a final round of ten minutes where people can share 'what's live in their thinking', before transitioning out of the space. This stage can also be a good time to undertake an appreciation round if there is time left, and the last round can end with everyone taking the time to say something positive about the person they are handing over to. This is a valuable tool for building trust, self-confidence, and professional relationships within the group.

## Action research as a means of CPD

To support staff in their progression and CPD, action research by both staff and students will be undertaken. This will allow for the sharing of evidence-based practice amongst each other and the wider peer group that is worked with. By using action research as a process of professional development, the organisation will be able to develop a culture where theory is continually integrated and feedback is collected on an ongoing basis by students and colleagues. It also shows students your role modelling and commitment to life-long learning, with both students and teaching teams learning alongside one another.

Action research allows for exploration of the *why* and *how* of what is undertaken. It also enables the organisation to lead educational research and share with others the high-quality work of its team. One- to three-year research projects are recommended, along with short ones that focus on particular aspects of the programme. A dedicated area on the team's communication platform would be developed to share findings and further information on the range of research projects. This will also include spaces to share reading material that colleagues have found useful, and staff may wish to upload their own video logs or blog-style entries to update the team on their findings.

On review of the underpinning values, *personal* falls under this. We do not want a clone of teachers on the team who are all doing things in the same way. Instead, we want to recognise the qualities and strengths of individuals, and it is important to recognise the importance of following staff's interests in how professional development and research are approached. If staff are enabled to follow their interests, you will gain a wealth of areas being analysed in detail, building on the collaborative strength of the team and building a culture of learning and communication.

**Staff master classes**

Throughout the year, staff will be encouraged to share their own expertise with each other through a series of masterclasses. The programme can be developed in advance for each semester, alongside ad-hoc sessions where someone has something new they would like to try out/share with others. The calendar should be accessible to all, and arrangements should be made for cover so that all who want to attend can. The masterclasses can focus on any area of education: subject-specific learning, well-being, teaching strategies, etc. This is a great way to create a more open environment and encourage the team to try something new with the knowledge that their colleagues are there to support them and will refrain from judgement or criticism. This area comes back to the team's dedication to lifelong learning and provides a simple mechanism for sharing ideas that have enhanced the classroom experience.

**Meetings of purpose**

Frequently, meetings are overcome by the intense needs of individual students. Although teaching, learning, and assessment are on the agenda, by the time you reach this agenda item, the opportunity for sharing practice and ideas has been lost due to time restraints or demands. Teaching, learning, and assessment should still be covered within team meetings in line with the setting, but having meetings solely focused on planning and delivery supports the team to create projects in more authentic and purposeful ways. Before heading to a meeting, consider its purpose. We may need to create time in the diary prior to attending to plan out what we want to review and create communication channels to pull content together as a group before meeting face-to-face. This often leads to less time together in the physical meeting, but the time is used more effectively with better outcomes.

**Thinking spaces**

Spaces do not always need to be ones where staff are together. The use of social media, online forums, and pin boards can provide a way of connecting staff to think together when they are working separately. If I see a hand-out left on a table as I enjoy my coffee break, the chances are I will pick it up to see what it says. Small snippets of ideas can be a great addition to the staff room. Online chat channels are an effective way for staff to share ideas and practice, as well as identify areas they feel they need support with. This is also an important extension for the physical classroom for students, and there should be spaces created for the learners to collate their reflections and ideas on the projects they are working on.

## Reading groups

With the amount of time we spend on screens, it is important to find a balance. Opportunities for students and staff to read bring much learning that will benefit studies and practice, whilst also providing us with a quiet space to focus. Reading group sessions should be held monthly, and even if individuals have not had the opportunity to read the book, they should still be encouraged to attend so that they can learn together and hear from others what they gained from the content. The initial sessions should be led by staff, and as the students begin to feel more confident, they can then take on the facilitation of this if they feel comfortable doing so. These sessions allow both students and educators to explore books and learn together. It is in this approach that we develop spaces where the power imbalance between educators and students is removed and the learners see that we are committed to learning with them. It is also a nice way to enjoy informal reflection together and build on a positive culture.

Time for quiet reading should also be incorporated into weekly lessons. This has stemmed from my own action research and the findings that quiet time is appreciated by students and brings a deeper understanding of the topics we are working on. PBL is serious; it can often be stereotyped as an approach with a lack of structure and that is somewhat chaotic, but this is far from the case. Reading not only brought great advantage to students' understanding of topics but also to their well-being. With a busy routine both in class and at home, we often feel like we need to be doing something productive, and reading is not always considered a way to do that. Switching off for 20 minutes to read in silence prevents us from skimming a webpage and not digesting the information in front of us. In the 20 minutes of reading time, there should be no distractions, and technology should be turned off/put away. It is up to the students to decide what they want to read, but they should have access to the library before commencing the session. If reading the same text, there should not be pressure on how much is read in the time period; this space should be an easy, non-pressurised time where students can feel relaxed. Teachers should refrain from working on other tasks at this time (step away from the emails.!) and read alongside the group. There is a lot to be said for our own well-being and enjoying the time to read a book that will support our own learning, and the transition out of the quiet time should be used for the group to reflect together on a summary of what they have learned from the text and what has left them curious as they progress on with the day.

## Hybrid working

It is important not to make assumptions about hybrid teaching. Not all of the students and teachers will feel confident in using the different delivery, facilitation, and learning strategies. They may also have difficulty with access arrangements, and although our world is surrounded by technology, we need to remember that we are not all at the same stage with how we access technological resources. This should be something that is not only considered at the start of the academic year but also as the programme evolves. Through the different staff sessions, these spaces build staff confidence in their approaches to hybrid learning, and it is highly important that a culture of collaboration is created. If you are choosing to adopt a hybrid model, consider as a team what its purpose is and how it will engage students in their learning experience.

**Annual week of creativity**

With the introduction of a vast range of projects, it is important for the student's findings and work to be celebrated and recognised. A week dedicated in the calendar to creativity and creative thinking will allow students to lead workshops, showcase their work to the wider community, and also access in-house/external training. This also allows for opportunities for the college to publicise the innovative and creative aspects of college culture. In the final chapter of this book, we will look in more detail at the importance of celebrating students' achievements, and I would encourage you to draw on this further when putting together your plans for your week of creativity. A week focused on creativity builds excitement, engagement, and responsibility and needs to be led by the students on how this will look within your setting.

**Beyond four walls**

This will be integral to the work on the *Alexandrite Educational Programme*. Educational settings are very much community spaces, where students gain the skills and knowledge needed for a vast range of subjects. Without opening up the door of the classroom, it is impossible to fully prosper. As a team, you need to first reflect on how the classroom is viewed. We have come to understand in education that learning spaces do not only need to be within the physical building, and it is important to provide students with information on how they can develop learning areas within their homes for home learning activities and also where we can learn together as a group away from our indoor area. There should also be more reflection on where learning takes place within the grounds of your educational setting. The outdoors should be seen as a learning space, along with local outdoor spaces. Walking tutorials should be used on a regular basis, and there should be focus before you leave the classroom on what you will be reflecting on. Small cue cards can be given to students ten minutes before you head outside, and they can discuss these with you, the educator, alongside their peers. Talking side-by-side with students about areas they are finding challenging can create a much more open dialogue, as it removes the intensity of discussing these across a desk. Returning to projects after some downtime also creates focus and good energy to progress with.

## Team teaching

PBL should take a holistic approach to subject areas where possible. This is not always realistic with subject-specialist lessons, but with advanced planning, educators are able to consider which aspects of the projects they will be responsible for facilitating. The open door policy of your organisation should extend to lessons, and there should be opportunities for teachers to teach collaboratively to support each other and the projects the students are working on. A review each term should consider how this will look and the benefits it can bring to delivery. Literacy and mathematical and digital skills have a large and relevant focus in Western education, and it is important to consider how these can be integrated into creative and innovative lessons that provide students with a holistic approach to the curriculum.

## Project-based learning

It may be surprising how much is considered with the *#AlexandriteEDPRO* before we move to PBL, but this model is a holistic approach that focuses not only on the educational elements but also on the culture of the communities that adopt it. As we have reviewed in previous chapters, flow and scaffolding are important to build students' confidence in leading projects, and by implementing the different elements, staff will feel empowered to facilitate PBL.

The curriculum needs to be designed with a range of projects. The first step will be to identify some of the core projects to be undertaken and map these to the relevant assessment criteria within the student's qualification. It should be clear what the projects are and how they will form the basis of the students' assessment and portfolio of learning. If PBL activities have been undertaken in previous years, these need to be reviewed to ensure they are still relevant and authentic to the new group that will be using them. Previous projects that have been successful should be evaluated to consider how to strengthen them moving forward, and it can be beneficial to meet with representatives from the awarding bodies with whom you work to gain their guidance on how the projects will meet their quality assurance process. Not all of the projects have to be large-scale; in fact, a range of smaller ones will be designed to allow students to show adaptability and teamwork throughout their studies. It will also support the design of a range of resources and activities that they will be able to take with them as they progress into employment within the sector. Students will keep a reflective journal of their learning across projects, which will allow for clear reflection on their journey throughout the year and their progression. As the academic years progress, educators and students may wish to build a bank of projects to work from, depending on their needs and focus. Pre-planned projects would be beneficial for periods such as induction and for core areas of learning. Sometimes there is a belief that all projects need to be fully designed by the students, but they still require the bones to be designed by the facilitators to ensure they are meeting the curriculum and organisational requirements. The key is that the students have the lead in what takes place during the project and are able to design it in a way that suits their needs. A strong beginning, middle, and end are essential for creating momentum and structure for how this will look.

Some learning within the course should remain more traditional so that there is flexibility for educators to use a vast range of teaching skills, and the new courses that will be implemented will allow for a range of assessment methods to be applied. Embracing PBL is not about minimising the areas that underpin teachers' pedagogy but instead encouraging the team to develop what they are doing and make it more student-led and relevant to the projects they are working on.

**Curiosity questions**

Exploring what makes us curious is an important focus in *#AlexandriteED-PRO*. Teachers should pose questions throughout the day that encourage discussion and refrain from providing the answers from the outset. An example of this was when I was teaching students on an early years qualification about historical changes to childhood in our country. As the students were growing up in Northern Ireland, I was aware that this topic would bring up some big topics, and I wanted to refrain from any of my own subconscious biases impacting how the session would be delivered. I explained this to students and asked them to consider in groups how they felt their lives were different from those of their parents and why they felt this was the case. The next question was to spark curiosity in the conversation and to consider why these childhoods may have been experienced by children in England and the Republic of Ireland. Instead of presenting significant historical events that have shaped Northern Ireland, the students took the lead in researching these and bringing them back to a group discussion that was underpinned with respect and trust. This lesson proved very moving to me as an educator and led down many lines of inquiry that we could shape into projects. Questions can be simple (what is childhood?) to be more complex (why are our experiences of childhood different across time and place?). But the important factor is to encourage students to embrace their investigative nature and feel engaged with the learning material.

**Assessment**

How students present their evidence will be largely led by them. Educators need to think differently about how students' work may be presented, and encouraging the students to evaluate how their projects are best presented is an important aspect for consideration. The annual week of creativity will be beneficial for showcasing final projects, and video logs that have taken place throughout the year can be pulled together for this final showcase. Presentations of projects this week can also form part of the assessment, but it is also important that assessment take place from the beginning to consider how learning can be scaffolded and supported by you as the educator. The arts and dialogue should be embraced as assessment methods, and students should also consider how their work could be used in a vocational or real-world context outside of the classroom.

# 13 Celebrating the successes and achievements that have been made through project-based learning

I still have my level three portfolio from when I began my apprenticeship to work in the early years sector. It is a big lever arch file with Tigger, from Winnie the Pooh, on its cover, and it reminds me of happy memories of working with a great team of adults and children. On each page, I see my employment supervisor's signature, confirming I carried out the duties recorded on the page. That supervisor soon became a wonderful friend and is now the godmother to my children. It is nice to reflect back and consider how she has supported me both personally and professionally in my working life. As I flick through the pages, the shape of the portfolio is not unlike many that I review frequently in my role now as a lecturer. There are knowledge-based assignments, reflective diary entries, and reports written up by my course assessor, who came out to see me in practice. It is nice to read over her feedback and see how my knowledge progressed as I moved through the course. The file now sits in a cupboard in my study and has been seen only by a few persons. The work-based supervisor reviewed it, the assessor reviewed it to mark off the learning criteria, and I saw it as I created it and after my evidence was returned. I presume there were other staff and verifiers who provided further checks to make sure quality procedures had been followed.

Nowadays, many of the students I work with have their portfolios online. It is the same process in many ways, but their evidence is uploaded into cyberspace for teachers to mark, and feedback is returned to them on the screen. Of course, verbal feedback comes throughout this process, but this does lead to much of the dialogue taking place on the virtual platform. Once work is signed off, it is rarely seen again. If we consider how we celebrate students' achievements, this does not lend itself to much celebration. Within this chapter, we will explore ways that we can close our PBL activities by recognising the successes of both groups and individuals. With students producing products to share with others, there are numerous ways that these successes can be presented to a wider audience and lead to further learning for the participants.

DOI: 10.4324/9781003424345-14

## Whole-setting events

I previously wrote about Michaela Greaves in Chapter 11 and her experiences with project-based learning (PBL) in the further education environment. Michaela's interview was a reminder of the importance of celebrating students' achievements. Michaela stressed how important it was to her and the teams she works with for students to have fun when learning alongside teachers and how this develops a love of learning and a commitment to studies. The 'Be Curious' Fair that was held midway through the year focused on staff's action research, but their grand finale was an event for both staff and students, with students able to showcase their learning and present it to others. Michaela is honest that organising an event of this size takes commitment from the team, and it was hard work to review all the logistics, but she stresses that this work was well worth it and everyone comes away incredibly proud by the end of the event. Students are not only showing their achievements to their peers in other curriculum areas, but others have also been invited, such as representatives from the awarding bodies and local employers. Students will see themselves in the local press following the event, with the press invited to talk with students and take photographs, and this is a wonderful way to promote the work completed by the staff team whilst also identifying the skills and knowledge of the student groups to the community. Incentives have been agreed upon by the college, and those projects that show the impact their sustainability project has had can receive a cash prize for further sustainability projects, books, and resources. In feedback to the College Board of Governors, a student provided feedback that

> The sustainability celebration day was an amazing day where students shared their learning, we learned from each other across departments! Can we please do more events like this as we loved the experience and our knowledge of Sustainability was improved greatly on the day.

The most important area that this day brings in Michaela's opinion though, is it provides the opportunity for students to shine. The impact this can have on students' confidence and self-esteem as they move into employment and transition into new chapters must be recognised.

## Alexandrite EDPRO week of creativity

An example of how the *Alexandrite EDPRO* week of creativity runs is outlined in the following, but it is important to work as a team (with both students and staff) to reflect on how the week can be best-shaped to suit your setting. It is important to consider what sparks curiosity in students and follow their lead so that the week is a success and truly embraces creativity.

Within the week, it is not just creativity that is embraced but also creative thinking, which is a fundamental skill for PBL.

| *Monday* | *Tuesday* | *Wednesday* | *Thursday* | *Friday* |
|---|---|---|---|---|
| PBL workshop on your chosen theme | Well-being and health | Environmental workshops | Messy learning | Final showcase and celebratory day |

**Monday:** Once the theme of your week has been agreed upon, workshops should be arranged for day one for students of different year groups/vocational areas to use blue-sky thinking to come up with an answer to the question the workshop poses. This should be a big question, and it should draw on the values of your setting. An example of this could be: 'What could our school do to meet the UN sustainable goal of protecting nature?' and students should spend time throughout the day exploring why this is a global and school priority before putting together their own designs, with the senior management team actively engaged with these. An agreement in advance for an allocated amount of projects to be implemented following the creativity week should be reached so that students know that their voice is listened to and that their ideas are valued. The first day will aim to grow both settings and learning experiences, engaging students in the events of the week.

**Tuesday**: Following a creative theme, the focus on the second day should be on well-being and health. Activities that encourage movement and social engagement help to build on pupils' emotional and physical health and act as a reminder of the importance of slowing down the routine so that we take care of ourselves. There should be no shaming on this day; instead, sessions on the importance of taking care of ourselves with practical examples of how to do this. Each day, students should be inputting into the leadership of the sessions, and they may wish to run sessions that are based around the physical hobbies they enjoy or provide a workshop on an area such as 'using social media positively for our mental health' or 'strategies for looking after our mental health at school'. Sessions outdoors can be led on nature journaling or using reflection for personal growth, and sitting outside to write and draw in our school diaries will be a reminder of the importance of understanding our feelings and how these impact our school day. Students can also be involved with the implementation by hosting a healthy lunch where school-grown produce is part of the menu or by adopting a meat-free menu. All of these student-led sessions can form part of an earlier project, with this being their end product and presentation.

**Wednesday:** You may have already touched on environmental concerns on day one, but this session should explore them further with workshops led by the students and teachers on the importance of taking care of our planet. Big questions should be posed, and you will benefit from getting guest speakers in to discuss their own work in the field. Keeping it relevant to your own community will help students reflect on what they can do to make a difference, as will the creative writing sessions being held on this day where students can write about a particular topic that is important to them in this area and share it with peers. Students should be viewed as future leaders, and consideration can be given as to how different job roles should take into account the environmental factors, which lead to a school debate and a set of pledges for the year ahead. It is important for a large period of the day to be spent outside, whether this is on your school grounds or in spaces that can be used in your local area.

**Thursday:** Your focus on the fourth day is to prepare for their final showcase whilst embracing messy learning. Using your week's theme, students should have access to different creative materials and be encouraged to use these to enhance the setting's environment. This is a great way to make school displays more relevant to learning and have students take the lead on what is displayed in classrooms. It is also important for students to work towards their showcase piece projects that they will present on the final day, using the materials to pull together their work and present it to a wider audience. Embracing creative thinking, workshops that utilise Lego and technology will also be great additions to the day to encourage students to use different resources for formulating and presenting their ideas. Using outdoor spaces is a big part of the week, and again, time should be spent outside for students to engage in sessions and use nature as a stimulant for ideas for their final day. By the end of the day, students will be ready to relax into the final day of the week of creativity, and their projects will be ready to be shared with others.

**Friday:** The final day should be a real celebration, with parents, families, and stakeholders invited in to share in the joy of learning and achievements. This event is very much led by the students, and they will have decided how their projects will be presented throughout the day. There may be poster presentations, videos, speakers, practical examples of what the students have made, and informal discussions over breaks that visitors can call into. The celebration should draw on your setting's values and appreciate all of the students' contributions, not just the chosen few. You may wish to have some of your external partners from the various projects talk at this event, sharing how students' contributions and involvement have supported their team. Throughout the week, you should have a student team assigned to capturing the learning that has taken place through the week of creativity, and during this last day, they can have time to share this with the attending audience. The record of the week should embrace the creativity that has taken place, and the students may wish to share this using a storyboard, animation, photography, or storytelling.

Planning any event requires commitment and positivity, and there may be challenges to having the whole setting involved (if you return to Chapter 6, this reviews how to overcome many barriers), but having students take ownership of the events of the week will widen the support network and ensure that individuals have clear roles and know what they need to do to make it a success. Having the senior management team on side and updating all parties throughout the planning stage will help everyone understand its purpose and encourage everyone to be involved. Whilst I appreciate that we have a curriculum to follow and time can be tight to deliver it, this week does not throw out the activities that are required but, instead, reminds us to use new strategies to deliver this and supports us with adopting a whole-child/student approach that considers both academic and emotional growth.

**Reframing priorities**

Affolter (2005) argues that a different type of universal goal should be constructed, which, instead of focusing on children's socio-economic development, should instead be creating policies that focus on children's socio-emotional well-being. This area is currently overlooked in global legislative frameworks and was not included as a priority area within the UN Millennium Goals, even though it is argued to be vital for children's confidence in their identity and positive belonging. Affolter (2005) concludes that the social security of communities in countries should be the focus and that the United Nations Convention on the Rights of the Child (UNCRC) pushes individuals away from this, prioritising goals for them to be economically active instead. With this in mind, our educational systems may have the wrong focus when concentrating on supporting pupils' growth, and children's socio-emotional development should be the targeted area due to it underpinning the other areas of children's development. This approach would allow children to be more actively involved in their experiences, as policies and practices would have to take into account their voice and feelings. Many of us do not have the ability to change the focus of policy on a global scale, but we are in a position to reflect on what we can do to support children's socio-emotional well-being. The purpose of this chapter is not just to discuss the importance of bringing projects to a close but also to consider how we can celebrate the values of your setting and the individuals within it and build on the pupils' well-being as they progress through their academic journey. We know that we have a crisis with mental health in our educational systems at the moment. Young people are struggling more and more with the pressures that surround them, and statistics show us that mental health is causing extreme pain in our children's lives. In the United Kingdom, one in six children, aged between 5 and 15, was identified as having a probable mental health problem in 2021 (NHS Digital). As an educator, I have seen how the worries and concerns of students have changed over the last decade, and the lack of services we have to support them in this area saddens me when it is so desperately required. I do not diminish the need to work towards academic achievement, but the importance of embedding mental health into our curriculum is now an essential element of the job. We need to ensure that a holistic approach to classroom experiences is adopted and that growth in all areas of development is celebrated.

## Teacher CPD

Inviting other teachers from your own setting to see the final projects not only promotes confidence in the students you work with, but it also works as a catalyst for connections to be made across the team. The final presentation is beneficial for students and serves as an opportunity for professional learning for the educators involved. Being open to questions and debate about the way you have facilitated the project can support growth both within yourself and for your colleagues. This can be something that should be embraced throughout projects, with teachers partaking in team teaching when possible and discussing progress in meetings and discussion time. The more open and trusting your organisation is, the more opportunities there are for learning from one another.

## Archiving projects

Reflecting on how you can maintain information on previous projects can help you inspire future students whilst also providing a mechanism for past students to reflect back and share their achievements. Digital platforms can prove a great way to do this, and I have seen online art galleries and video reflections used to gather final products into one space. Encouraging students to record their advice on how they approached their work and how they overcame challenges will be a beneficial addition for future cohorts.

Connections with your local media outlets can be a great way to share information on a wider scale. Keeping a catalogue that brings together articles and news bites from your projects not only provides inspiration but is also a lovely way to see how much has been achieved by pupils in your setting.

## Appreciation for students

There is a lot to be said for a personalised letter sent through the mail. Postcards of appreciation that recognise students' contributions not only provide them with a boost in confidence and show that you care, but they can also act as a prompt for conversations about children's learning at home. Taking 15 minutes to send some personalised postcards home that value the contributions of individuals is an easy way to embed positive mental health strategies into your delivery.

## Working in partnership with families

Families that play an active role in their children's learning can have a significant impact on their development. Inviting families to end-of-project events builds partnerships and provides insight into their child's school day.

The Education Endowment Foundation (2021, p. 41) reports that parent engagement in education has a positive impact on an average of four months of additional progress. Parents and carers play a paramount role in children's learning and development. Having a project where students put together a school newsletter or blog that runs throughout projects can be used to interact with families online, with a function for them to add comments and feedback in response to students' articles included. As parents and families see the progress of the projects, their engagement at the end of project events will be heightened as they have been involved from the outset in their children's learning activities.

As a working mum, I can appreciate how hard it can be to juggle the diary and attend school events. Scheduling these days, in advance, at the start of the year is a good way to encourage parents and carers to attend, outlining the purpose of these days alongside information as to how they can help their children with project work. Consideration of timing can also widen the commitment parents can have to event days, and it may suit your school community to have ones planned in the evenings if staff members are in agreement. I have attended some lovely outdoor projects where parents are invited in for a barbecue or tea party at the weekend, with information shared on their younger child's learning in an informal environment. I have also seen staff choosing to host part of their outdoor learning projects earlier in the project, encouraging parents to become involved by sharing their expertise with the pupil group and sprucing up the playground area, ready for the children's plans to be implemented.

**Displays**

When you look at your classroom displays, what enhancement do they bring to students learning and/or well-being? As discussed earlier in this chapter in relation to the week of creativity, encouraging students to take the lead on what is displayed can not only form part of the learning process but can also be used as part of their final evidence. Poster displays and visual curiosity prompts can be ways to utilise wall features. With technology becoming more integrated into classrooms, you may also wish to use pictorial displays that show previous projects on a video stream. Consideration needs to be given to where displays are physically placed; boards at adult height are of little use to young children who need to crane their necks to see them. Photos of past students' achievements through their project work can show current groups a positive role model and provide an aspirational incentive to work towards a similar goal. Pop-up displays and ones that children can interact with and adapt are also useful. Showing the journey of a project throughout the year is a beneficial way of evidencing pupils' progression and learning. Moving away from laminated, end-product displays that are neatly bordered can have a positive impact on how students interact with their environment.

## Social media

In 2022, I received an award from the Northern Ireland Social Media Awards for 'Best Use of Social Media' in Education. Not only was this a good feeling to have the work I had put into the various channels recognised, but it was also a great boost to the students who are involved in the content. I generally use Twitter to connect with other educators, and I use Facebook as an extension of our classroom. Students are able to share their projects and learning, with many local employers and stakeholders engaging with their posts. The page is also used to share blogs and learning content as part of our blended learning activities, and by sharing them publicly, the opportunity for discussion is widened. This platform creates a space for us to raise the professional profile of the sector we work in whilst providing the students with links to future employers. Frequently, businesses and organisations have been part of our projects and are able to see students share their final projects, acting as an extension of their curriculum vitae. It builds the name of our organisation and, in turn, develops an awareness of the skills and knowledge of the students who have studied with us. Alongside that, it is a source of pride, with students frequently showing their families what they have been doing at college, building on the connection and support mechanism between education and home. As we have moved through this book, we have explored the importance of recognising emotions and building students' self-confidence. Students seeing comments from external voices praising their work is a great catalyst for developing students' confidence in their ability as they begin to recognise that their voice has value. Evaluating how you can use social media to share ideas and showcase students' participation can widen the connections students have in a positive way and also share students' learning with others. There have been some great collaborative projects put in place with both other similar organisations to my own and with stakeholders who can support us with a project focus thanks to being visible and active on social media in a professional capacity.

## Transitioning to university and employment

When supporting students in their university applications, their personal statements include details on some of the projects that they have developed. It is with ease that we are able to draw on experiences where students have been able to display leadership skills, innovation, and creativity – skills asked for from students as they progress into higher education. Students are confident in being researchers and understand the need to be critical thinkers, something that is often not a focus until degree level in education. There were many times before embedding PBL that we found it tricky to fully showcase the student in the short application, which is sent to reflect their educational and personal experiences. The projects provide us with clear, outcome-based activities that the student has led us to write about, with an awareness of their responsibilities within this and how the project benefited others. The same is applicable when students are completing job applications and interviews. They have already gained experience with the knowledge and skills that will be required for the professional role, putting them in a strong position for employment.

**The importance of closure**

In the field of employment, when a project comes to an end, the employer will be provided with feedback as to whether the end outcome is satisfactory, and consideration will be given as to how it will fit within the current models of working. That feedback is essential for determining if targets and outcomes were achieved. Just as important for us as educators is to provide students with feedback for growth and development. Explaining to students where they have excelled in the project and providing kind and constructive feedback leads them on the path of being lifelong learners and recognising the importance of education. When projects dwindle and are not appropriately closed, individuals lose interest and will think that there was little purpose for their efforts. The reasoning for having proper closure for projects is incredibly important and ensures that, even if the next project takes on aspects of what has been learned before, it is something new that requires the students' full attention. If we want students to be adaptable, forward-thinking, and dynamic, we need them to be able to use past learning and knowledge to create something new. Building their confidence in their own ability and showing them what has been achieved in short periods of time will enable each individual to recognise how their own skills and expertise have developed and evaluate how these can be adapted for future goals.

# Conclusion

When I was a young girl, one of my favourite movies to watch was *The Blues Brothers*. My father and I would watch it on repeat, singing along to the music, and, when I play it back now, I still pretty much know every word. Quick disclaimer: This movie is totally inappropriate for children, but I was an 80s child, so enough said! My father died young in life so the movie does bring a great sense of nostalgia for me, taking me back to snuggling up on the sofa and working out the underpinning morals that run through the script. The movie starts with the two brothers meeting with the nun who cared for them in their childhood and her disclosing how much financial trouble the children's home they grew up in is having. They tell her they will get the money, but she becomes angry that they will do this through illegal means, and she tells them to go and redeem themselves. As the movie continues, the brothers try to prove themselves to the nun whilst raising money to save the home. The movie was probably my first introduction to overcoming large obstacles. *The Blues Brothers* sing their way across Chicago and get the money to the county office just before the papers are signed to repossess the property.

There is a lot of theory in this book, and I want to emphasise that my conclusion is not based on the highly illegal nature of progressing through life (!!), but I do find myself smiling as I find myself linking the movie to my own pedagogical practice and parenting style. When there is a problem or a sticky situation, there is a way to find a solution. I struggle most in life when I feel trapped and I see no solution to a problem. When people share their worries, it is so important to listen; that is what is needed in that moment for the individual to feel secure. From there, it can then be worthwhile to explore what can be done, and when my own children come to me with a problem, that's very often one of the first questions I ask them: 'So what can we do now to fix this?'. Sometimes the listening has been enough. They have worked out their own solution. Sometimes they need support, and that's where teamwork comes in – whether it be from us, their parents, or the wider community that surrounds them. And then there's the curiosity. These inquiries are not problems, but they still leave us needing to find out more about something we do not fully understand. The same process needs to take place; we need to sit back, reflect, and consider how we can find out the information that we desire. The information may not change the world or lead to any defined outcome, but it stimulates our minds and develops our skills as lifelong learners. It reminds us that learning does not need to be dull and can be undertaken for the sole purpose of finding satisfaction. The end of the movie sees their objective obtained, and the children's home stays open, but the men have left a trail of disaster behind them. This book gives us the ability to use play and curiosity in a refined way that only leaves possibilities surrounding us and a way to find ways to overcome obstacles, seeking out the knowledge we need for unanswered questions.

I spent a lot of time in France growing up. Every school holiday, the car would be packed up, and we would head across the water to Brittany. Now I have a similar routine with my own children, and as soon as I arrive, I find peace. Our family home there has a very special secret spot, and it takes us a little bit of work to find it after a season of overgrowth. Moving through the forest, there is a place with large granite stones, and over the years, it has changed, with trees growing larger around it, a pond there one year and disappearing the next before returning again. When I say this place is magic, I mean it, and I feel very lucky that there is a place consumed by nature that allows me to share its presence. Over the years, I have learned that all of my family has been taken in by its magic and found healing, reflection, and learning by being still in the space and leaving nature to guide them. Before the witch hunt starts and I go any further with my conclusion drawing on magical energy, I will now explain why the space brings reflection and ease to each of us.

Firstly, each of us switches off when we are there. Three generations of us go home, and it's our space to be away from the background noise that can distract us in our normal routine. When we get there, there are different jobs to do, and these mainly consist of spending time respecting nature and evaluating how we can spend time in unison with its rhythm. Paths are trampled down only as necessary, and we provide quiet warnings to the creatures in the woods that they have neighbours for a little while so as not to scare them. We try not to be scared by them, but we are in awe when we find a deer staring at us through the window as we wake up. This rhythm is so different from the one we usually find and reminds us of the importance of slowing down and being present with the elements. The feelings that it brings are probably one of the reasons why I value outdoor learning so much. My senses are heightened, and my well-being immediately improves.

Secondly, there are parts of this space that remain; for example, the granite rocks remain (to our eyes) the same, but around them, the years and the seasons bring a variety of changes. There have been years where the stones have vanished, consumed by the wilderness. Other years, where they stand proud and I can sit myself down on top of them. My learning is scaffolded; I see something new that I have not seen before. New growth develops that I do not recognise; this brings a challenge to my perspective.

Every sense is stimulated, and yet the space remains calm. The birds, used to being alone in their species, continue with their usual routine. To listen to them brings wonder; if you sit for a period of time, you start to home in on their conversations and recognise different bird songs. When I consider our learning spaces, the woodland reminds me to consider the importance of positive stimulants in our learning environment. Background noise and distractions are beneficial if they bring purpose to our learning experience and help us create focused calm.

Most importantly, the space leaves you be. You have to recognise your emotions whilst there, and I think this is where the real magic comes. When we slow down, we find our natural curiosities start to heighten, and we begin to explore our thinking whilst finding space to process our emotions and appreciate where they stem from. In a busy world, there can be little opportunity to sit comfortably with our feelings and truly understand what they mean. Quiet and independent reflection is often what brings this about.

I once wandered up to the space for some quiet time and found my middle daughter there. I stood back and observed her play, and when she noticed me, I got a smile, but her engagement in her play continued. She was deep into an investigation of water levels with a large branch and a firm footing on top of the standing stones. I sat back and observed. My daughter, content with my presence, was not ready for conversation, but after some time I felt able to ask if she would explain her line of inquiry. She continued and explained her investigation, asking how the landscape had changed since the summer before. I was invited to join, and I took her lead on how I could help. This was not a lesson built on googling information, reading a book, or even gaining the full answers she was after. Instead, it was time to make sense of her own experiences and see how nature responded to her experiments and investigations.

As someone who loves experimentation and play, technology sits high as a tool for me to experiment with, and I place great value on how it can enhance the learning experience. However, we are not built to sit in front of screens continuously, and, like everything in life, balance is required. My final reflections draw on the need to be present in the space we are in and consider how we can utilise the natural world to stimulate thinking and productivity. As someone who taught during the 2020 COVID-19 lockdown period, I had to reflect greatly on how classroom environments needed to be re-evaluated. As we went through our lessons, we were not in the same space and not always in similar environments; we incorporated the outdoors into our day and valued the importance of quiet spaces to reflect, along with agreeing ways to connect that suited our new routine. A full day of sitting at a desk from 9 a.m. to 3 p.m. was not realistic, and it brought us into consideration as to whether it had ever been. Curiosity requires stimulation; considering where you can move outside and connect with the community that surrounds you will strengthen your projects and ensure their authenticity and value.

This book calls for us to listen to our innate playful motivations. Play is not something we grow out of; it is often something that we suppress as it is seen as childish and not relevant in the adult world. My own adulthood is led by many playful interactions, from how I form relationships to how I put

112  *Conclusion*

*Figure 14.1* Fey's quiet place.

together my planning for a report, as well as the way in which I look after my emotional health. In adulthood, play is often much more disciplined in focus and calls for consideration to be given to how it is incorporated respectfully so that others feel comfortable with it. It is certainly not an activity to belittle individuals or the task at hand. Instead, it is to be valued as a highly purposeful way to learn that can support us in building self-confidence and belief in our abilities. I believe it is a necessary tool for future leaders and relevant for many industries that young people will later find themselves working in. As the book draws to a close, I ask you to be brave, embrace your playful nature, and get you and the students you work with outside, with spaces for open dialogue and a focus on the values important to all of the group. Being led by what we believe can open up a world of possibilities.

# References

## Chapter 1

Blackstock, C. (2011) 'The emergence of the breath of life theory', *Journal of Social Work Values and Ethics*, 8(1).

Bruner, J. S. (1961) The act of discovery. *Harvard Educational Review*, 31, pp. 21–32.

Bruner, J. S. (1986) *Actual minds, possible worlds*. Cambridge, MA: Harvard University Press.

DeVries, R. and Kohlberg, L. (1990) *Constructivist early education: Overview and comparison with other programs*. Washington, DC: National Association for the Education of Young Children.

Dewey, J. (2011) *Democracy and education*. London, England: Simon & Brown.

Eisenberg, D., Downs, M. and Golberstein, S. (2009) 'Stigma and help-seeking for mental health among college students', *Medical Care Research and Review*, 66(5), pp. 522–541.

Freire, P. (2017) *Pedagogy of the oppressed*. London, England: Penguin Classics.

Hanesworth, P., Bracken, S. and Elkington, S. (2019) 'A typology for a social justice approach to assessment: Learning from universal design and culturally sustaining pedagogy', *Teaching in Higher Education*, 24(1), pp. 98–114. https://doi.org/10.1080/13562517.2018.1465405

Huang, Y. -C. (2021) 'Comparison and contrast of Piaget and Vygotsky's theories', *Advances in Social Science, Education and Humanities Research*, 554(1), pp. 28–32, in Atlantis Press. https://doi.org/10.2991/assehr.k.210519.007.

Maslow, A. H. (1954) *Motivation and personality*. New York: Harper and Row.

Miraei, R. (2005) *The relationship between self-esteem, self-concept and academic achievement among junior high school students*. West Azerbaijan Province, Iran: University of Tarbiat Moallem.

Oxford, R. L. (1997) 'Cooperative learning, collaborative learning, and interaction: Three communicative strands in the language classroom', *The Modern Language Journal*, 81, pp. 443–456. https://doi.org/10.1111/j.1540-4781.1997.tb05510.x.

Piaget, J. (1964) 'Cognitive development in children: Development and learning', *Journal of Research in Science Teaching*, 2, pp. 176–186.

Rousseau, J. -J. (2004) *The social contract*. London, England: Penguin Books.

Vygotsky, L. S. (1978) *Mind in society: The development of higher psychological processes*. Cambridge, MA: Harvard University Press.

## Chapter 2

Belle, C. (2019) 'What is social justice education anyway?' *Education Week*, 23 January. Available at: www.edweek.org/teaching-learning/opinion-what-is-social-justice-education-anyway/2019/01.

Brown, B. (2013) *Daring greatly: How the courage to be vulnerable transforms the way we live, love, parent and lead.* London, England: Portfolio Penguin.

Cole, F. (2022) *Intergenerational learning in schools and settings: An educator's guide.* 1st edn. Oxen, England: Routledge Publication.

Counts, G. S. (1932) *Dare the school build a new social order.* Carbondale, IL: Southern Illinois University Press.

Elliott, L. (2023) 'Britain's working classes: A far cry from the 1840s', *The Guardian*, 5 June. Available at: www.theguardian.com/business/economics-blog/2013/jun/05/britains-working-classes-changes-since-1840s.

Freire, P. (2017) *Pedagogy of the oppressed.* London, England: Penguin Classics.

Gardner, J., Holmes, B. and Leitch, R. (2019) 'Assessment and social justice: A future lab literature review', *Future Lab*, 16. Available at: www.nfer.ac.uk/media/1826/futl63.pdf.

Hooks, B. (1994) *Teaching to transgress: Education as the practice of freedom.* London: Routledge.

Kline, N. (1998) *Time to think: Listening to ignite the human mind.* London: Cassell.

Office of National Statistics. (2023) 'Labour market overview, UK: December 2022', *Census 2021*, 17 January. Available at: www.ons.gov.uk/employmentandlabourmarket/peopleinwork/employmentandemployeetypes/bulletins/uklabourmarket/december2022.

Raelin, J. A. (2002) 'I don't have time to think!' (vs. The art of reflective practice). *Reflections*, 4(1) (Fall), pp. 66–79. Available at: https://ssrn.com/abstract=3190188.

The Skills Network. (2023) 'Skills gap trend report', *Emsi*, 10 January. Available at: https://theskillsnetwork-2348474.hs-sites.com/en/skills-gap-trend-report-b2b-2021.

Twenge, J., *et al.* (2010) 'Birth cohort increases in psychopathology among young Americans, 1938–2007: A cross-temporal meta-analysis of the MMPI. In press', *Clinical Psychology Review*, 30, pp. 145–154.

UK Parliament. (2023) *The 1870 education act.* Available at: www.parliament.uk/about/living-heritage/transformingsociety/livinglearning/school/overview/1870educationact/.

## Chapter 3

Gardner, J., Holmes, B. and Leitch, R. (2019) 'Assessment and social justice: A future lab literature review', *Future Lab*, 16. Available at: www.nfer.ac.uk/media/1826/futl63.pdf.

Lindsay, H. (2016) 'More than "continuing professional development": A proposed new learning model for professional accountants', *Accounting Education*, 25(1), pp. 1–13. Available at: https://www-tandfonline-com.libezproxy.open.ac.uk/doi/full/10.1080/09639284.2015.1104641.

Mehta, R., Henriksen, D., Mishra, P. *et al.* (2020) ' "Let children play!": Connecting evolutionary psychology and creativity with Peter Gray', *TechTrends*, 64, pp. 684–689. https://doi.org/10.1007/s11528-020-00535-y.

## Chapter 4

Csikszentmihalyi, M. (1990) *Flow: The psychology of optimal experience.* New York: Harper & Row.

Gettysburg College. (2023) *One third of your life is spent at work.* Available at: www.gettysburg.edu/news/stories?id=79db7b34-630c-4f49-ad32-4ab9ea48e72b.

Helgesen, S. (2008) 'The practical wisdom of Ikujiro Nonaka', *Strategy and Business*, 53 (Winter). Available at: www.strategy-business.com/media/file/sb53_08407.pdf.

Lindsay, H. (2016) 'More than "continuing professional development": A proposed new learning model for professional accountants', *Accounting Education*, 25(1), pp. 1–13. Available at: https://www-tandfonline-com.libezproxy.open.ac.uk/doi/full/10.1080/09639284.2015.1104641.

Mental Health Foundation. (2021) *Nature. How connecting with nature benefits our mental health.* Available at: www.mentalhealth.org.uk/sites/default/files/2022-06/MHAW21-Nature-research-report.pdf.

Pocock, M. J. O., Hamlin, I., Christelow, J., Passmore, H.-A. and Richardson, M. (2023) 'The benefits of citizen science and nature-noticing activities for well-being, nature connectedness and pro-nature conservation behaviours', *People and Nature*, 5, pp. 591–606. https://doi.org/10.1002/pan3.10432.

Tidball, K. G. (2012) 'Urgent biophilia: Human-nature interactions and biological attractions in disaster resilience', *Ecology and Society*, 17. https://doi.org/10.5751/ES-04596-170205.

Van den Berg, A. E., Wesselius, J. E., Maas, J. and Tanja-Dijkstra, K. (2017) 'Green walls for a restorative classroom environment: A controlled evaluation study', *Environment and Behavior*, 49(7), pp. 791–813. https://doi.org/10.1177/0013916516667976.

Walker, C. J. (2010) 'Experiencing flow: Is doing it together better than doing it alone?' *The Journal of Positive Psychology*, 5(1), pp. 5–11.

## Chapter 5

Anji Education. (2023a) *AnjiPlay: History.* Available at: www.anjiplay.com/overview.

Anji Education. (2023b) *AnjiPlay: Overview.* Available at: www.anjiplay.com/overview.

Duke, N. K., Halvorsen, A.-L., Strachan, S. L., Kim, J. and Konstantopoulos, S. (2021) 'Putting PBL to the test: The impact of project-based learning on second graders' social studies and literacy learning and motivation in low-SES school settings', *American Educational Research Journal*, 58(1), pp. 160–200. https://doi.org/10.3102/0002831220929638.

Edwards, C., Gandini, L. and Forman, G. (2012) *The hundred languages of children: The Reggio Emilia experience in transformation.* 3rd edn. Santa Barbara, CA: Praeger Press.

Li, H. and Rao, N. (2005) 'Curricular and instructional influences on early literacy attainment: Evidence from Beijing, Hong Kong and Singapore', *International Journal of Early Years Education*, 13(3), pp. 235–253.

Nemo, J. (2014) 'What a NASA janitor can teach us about living a bigger life', *The Business Journal*, 23 December. Available at: www.bizjournals.com/bizjournals/how-to/growth-strategies/2014/12/what-a-nasa-janitor-can-teach-us.html.

Nonaka, I. and Konno, N. (1998) 'The concept of "Ba": Building a foundation for knowledge creation', *California Management Review*, 40(3), pp. 40–54.

Available at: http://contents.kocw.net/KOCW/document/2014/Chungbuk/KimSangWook/10-1.pdf.

Nonaka, I. and Takeuchi, H. (1996) *The knowledge creating company; How Japanese companies create the dynamics of innovation*. Oxford, UK: Oxford University Press.

Pratt, C. (2014) *I learn from children: An adventure in progressive education*. New York: Grove Atlantic.

## Chapter 6

Criado Perez, C. (2019) *Invisible women: Data bias in a world designed for men*. London: Chatto and Windus.

Harbster, J. (2020) 'Margaret Rossiter and the Matilda effect', *Library of Congress Blogs*. Available at: https://blogs.loc.gov/inside_adams/2020/03/matilda-effect/.

## Chapter 7

Deleuze, G. and Guattari, F. (2004) *A thousand plateaus*. Translated by B. Massumi. London: Continuum.

## Chapter 8

O'Dell, L. (2010) 'Theorising development, constructing "normal" childhoods', in Robb, M. and Thompson, R. (eds.) *Critical practice with children*. University of Bristol, Bristol: The Policy Press.

Pratt, C. (2014) *I learn from children: An adventure in progressive education*. New York: Grove Atlantic.

Woodhead, M. (1999) 'Reconstructing developmental psychology – some first steps', *Children & Society*, 13(1), pp. 3–19. Available at: http://oro.open.ac.uk/35891/.

## Chapter 9

Howard, J. (2020) *How to make a wildlife pond*. Available at: www.countryfile.com/wildlife/make-a-wildlife-pond/.

IBO. (2023) *Primary years programme*. Available at: www.ibo.org/programmes/primary-years-programme/.

Woodhead, M. (1999) 'Reconstructing developmental psychology – some first steps', *Children & Society*, 13(1), pp. 3–19. Available at: http://oro.open.ac.uk/35891/.

## Chapter 10

APPG. (2021) *Speak for change*. Available at: https://oracy.inparliament.uk/files/oracy/2021-04/Oracy_APPG_FinalReport_28_04%20%284%29.pdf.

Battelle for Kids. (2023) *Frameworks & resources*. Available at: www.battelleforkids.org/networks/p21/frameworks-resources.

## Chapter 11

Cole, F. (2022) *Intergenerational learning in schools and settings: An educator's guide*. 1st edn. Oxen, England: Routledge Publication.

Meredith, R. (2023) 'Baby books: Stormont funding cuts end free scheme', *BBC News*. Available at: https://www.bbc.co.uk/news/uk-northern-ireland-65267207.

RCSLT NI. (2022) *NI independent review of education – Briefing from the royal college of speech and language therapists (RCSLT)*. Available at: www.rcslt.org/wp-content/uploads/2022/05/RCSLT-NI-briefing-Independent-Review-of-Education-May-22.pdf.

## Chapter 12

Kline, N. (1999) *Time to think: Listening to ignite the human mind*. London: Cassell.

Kline, N. (2009) *More time to think*. Pool-in-Wharfedale: Fisher King Pub.

Shephard, T. V., Lea, S. E. and Hempel de Ibarra, N. (2015) 'The thieving magpie? No evidence for attraction to shiny objects', *Animal Cognition*, 18(1), pp. 393–397. https://doi.org/10.1007/s10071-014-0794-4.

Syed, M. (2022) *Rebel ideas*. London, England: John Murray Press.

## Chapter 13

Affolter, F. (2005) 'Restricted access socio-emotional enablement and the convention of the rights of the child', *The International Journal of Children's Rights*, 13(3), pp. 379–397.

Education Endowment Foundation. (2021) *Parental engagement*. Available at: https://educationendowmentfoundation.org.uk/education-evidence/teaching-learning-toolkit/parental-engagement.

NHS Digital. (2021) *Mental health of children and young people in England 2021*. Leeds, England: NHS Digital.

# Index

accommodation 5, 8
action research 30, 35–36, 81–82, 93, 95, 101
Alexandrite Educational Programme 30, 83, 87–91, 96–98, 101
America 33, 44–45, 78
Anji 44
Anjiplay 44
Asia 7, 29, 33, 44
ASPIRE 81
assimilation 8
Association of Colleges 56, 60

*Ba* 41–42
Baccalaureate PYP 71
Beacon Awards for Social Action 56, 60
Bell, Crystal, Dr. 23
biophilia 34–35
Blackfoot 11–12
Blues Brothers 109
Book Trust 83
Brittany 110
Brown, Brene 20
Bruner, Jerome 9–10

Canada 11
Carr, Abigail 64
Chesterfield College 81
Chicago 12, 109
China 7, 44, 77–78
Chinese 44, 60, 65–66
Chung, Angela 51, 60, 71
classroom design 34–35
Cole, Fey 22, 67–68, 83
Confucius 7
constructivism 5–8, 10, 25
Covid-19 16–17, 34, 36, 64–66, 68, 87, 89–90, 111
Csikszentmihalyi, Mihaly 37–38

Deleuze & Guattari 56
democracy 13, 23
development, proximal 8–9
Dewey, John 12–13, 23

Education Training Foundation 81
Elementary Education Act, 1870 15
England 62, 72, 81, 98
English 41, 65–66, 73, 78
Enlightenment period 6
equilibrium 8–9
ethic of care 89
Europe 6, 44
Exeter University 88

Flow Theory 38
France 110
Freire, Paolo 6, 15
Froebel, Friedrich 67

Gage, Matilda Joslyn 53–54
Gettysburg College 38
Google 54–55
Gray, Peter, Dr. 26–27
Greaves, Michaela 80–82
Green Economy 17
Grimm Brothers 78

hierarchy of need 11–12
Hong Kong 29, 33, 51, 60–62, 64–66, 71–72
Hooks, Bell 21–22
Howard, Jules 72–73

Ideas Rooms 87–88, 91–93
India 33
intergenerational 1, 14, 22, 47–48, 56–57, 60, 62, 67, 79, 82–83
Ireland, Republic of 98

Japan 41–42
JoyFE 80–81, 87–88

Kennedy, John F., President 45
Kindness Postbox 68
Kline, Nancy 87–88, 92
Koru 66

Laboratory School 12–13
learning, active 10–13, 66
learning as becoming 40
learning, collaborative 9–10
learning, discovery 10–11
learning, lifelong 3, 12, 29, 40, 77, 94, 108, 110
learning, outdoor 35–36, 41–42, 81, 106, 110
learning, spiralling 20–21, 42–43, 66
learning walks 35–36, 47
Lego 27, 45, 103
Li & Rao 44
Lindsay, Hilary 30, 40
lock-down *see* Covid-19
London 26, 33

Malaguzzi, Loris 43–44
management 16–17, 78–79, 85, 102, 104
Maori 66
Maslow, Abraham 11–12
Matilda Effect, The 53–54
Mental Health Foundation 35
Meredith, Robbie 83
Miraei 13–14
Montessori, Maria 5, 61
Mycroft, Lou, Dr. 87

NASA 45
Netherlands 34
neurodiversity 35
New York 39
Nishida, Kitaro 41–42
Nonaka & Konno 41–42
Nonaka & Takauchi 41–42
Northern Ireland 3, 33–34, 60, 78, 83–84, 87, 98, 107
Northern Ireland Department of Education 83

O'Dell, Lindsay 64
Oracy All-Party Parliamentary Group 75
O'Toole, Nuala 68

Pandemic *see* Covid-19
Perez, Caroline Criado 49

Piaget, Jean 5, 7–9
Play Association 44
Practice of Freedom 16
Pratt, Caroline 43, 66–67

Queen's Award 62

RCSLT NI 83–84
Reardon-James, Anne 46
River Valley 11–12
Rossiter, Margaret W. 53
Rousseau, Jean-Jacques 67

Saskatchewan 11–12
scaffolding 9–10
schema 8–9
SECI model 42–43
Shukie, Peter 62
Skills Gap Trend Report 16
skills, green 17
skills, learning 74–75
skills, life 74, 76
skills, literacy 75–76
social construct 10, 64
*social media* 16, 18, 29, 48, 58–59, 67, 79, 91, 94, 102, 107
Spain 33
Spiegelman, Art 78
Syed, Matthew 87–88

thinking environment 87, 92–93
thinking pairs 92
Tinsley, Stephanie 87
Twenge, Jean 18

UK Centre for Ecology and Hydrology 34
UK *see* United Kingdom
United Kingdom 15, 28–29, 61, 64–65, 69, 71–72, 77–78, 80, 83, 92, 104
United Nations Sustainable Goals 79
University of Chicago 12

Vygotsky, Lev 5, 7–9

Wales 46
Walker, Charles 38
WEA, Social Impact Award 62
White, E. B. 78
Woodhead, Martin 64, 70

Xueqin, Cheng 44

For Product Safety Concerns and Information please contact our EU representative  GPSR@taylorandfrancis.com
Taylor & Francis Verlag GmbH, Kaufingerstraße 24, 80331 München, Germany

www.ingramcontent.com/pod-product-compliance
Lightning Source LLC
Chambersburg PA
CBHW052026290426
44112CB00014B/2401